Reading Comprehension Test Taking Skills Grade 7

Best Value Books™

by
Patricia Pedigo
and
Dr. Roger DeSanti

ISBN 0-88724-480-7

Table of Contents

About the book

This book is just one in our Best Value™ series of reproducible, skill-oriented activity books. Standardized tests have become a typical means of student achievement evaluation. Many students may not perform as well as they might on these tests simply due to a lack of practice in test taking and/or a lack of understanding of the task presented. This book is designed to provide practice activities for appropriate application of reading comprehension and test taking strategies.

The passages presented in this book cover a variety of word skills and real reading situations including narrative, expository, directions, and letters. The passage questions are presented in a typical standardized testing format that targets specific levels of comprehension (literal, inferential, applied, and prediction or judgmental). Each level of comprehension calls for different strategies that are discussed in detail on the pages titled "Levels of Comprehension." It is the authors' contention that children should be made aware of these levels of comprehension and the associated strategies for each. Providing the children with these comprehension tools gives them an organized approach to answering questions about any given passage.

Also included in this book is a list of Test Taking Tips for students, found on page vi. This list includes many strategies that may be helpful in a variety of test taking situations (true and false, multiple choice, and matching).

About the authors

Patricia Pedigo has many years of teaching experience in urban, rural, public, and private settings. She has taught all elementary and middle school grade levels and has been a reading specialist. While teaching at the University of New Orleans, Patricia professed her belief in finding creative ways to teach through practical applications. She has created many materials that incorporate a reading approach integrating content areas and language development. She holds an M.Ed. in Reading Education.

Dr. Roger DeSanti has been an educator since the mid 1970's. His teaching experiences have spanned a wide range of grade and ability levels from deaf nursery through university graduate school. As a professor, he has authored numerous articles and books, achievement tests, and instructional materials.

Levels of Comprehension

There are many levels at which we may comprehend text, ranging from very simple to deeply complex. There are several different models of comprehension that demonstrate these levels in a detailed manner. However, we found that a simple version of these models is most effective with children. Below is a short passage followed by a discussion of four levels of comprehension, example questions, and strategies to employ when answering the questions.

Ben sat on the front steps. His chin was cupped in his hand and tears were trickling down his cheeks. On the step beside Ben lay a leash with the name "Rags" embossed on the leather. Ben had looked everywhere he could think, but it was no use.

Literal

Literal comprehension is an understanding of what has been clearly stated in the passage. Questions that require literal comprehension will ask for information that has been given. For example:

1. What is the name of the boy in this story? (Ben)
2. Where is Ben sitting? (on the front steps)
3. What is on the step next to Ben? (a leash)

The best strategy for answering literal comprehension questions is simply to look back at the text and find the answer.

Inferential

Inferential comprehension is the ability to understand the implied message of the text. Questions that require inferential comprehension will ask for information that is suggested but never directly stated in the text. For example:

1. How is Ben feeling? (sad)

To answer an inferential comprehension question the reader needs to find clues that imply the meaning. For the example question, it is necessary to look at the stated information that gives a hint as to how Ben may be feeling. The example states that Ben's "chin was cupped in his hand," a behavior that usually accompanies boredom or sadness. The second clue given is that "tears were trickling down his cheeks." These two pieces of information imply that Ben is sad.

Levels of Comprehension

Ben sat on the front steps. His chin was cupped in his hand and tears were trickling down his cheeks. On the step beside Ben lay a leash with the name "Rags" embossed on the leather. Ben had looked everywhere he could think, but it was no use.

Applied

Applied comprehension requires that the reader use the stated and implied information and apply it to what he/she already knows about such situations. This level of comprehension takes the reader beyond the text and into his/her own knowledge base. For example:

1. Who is Rags? (a dog, cat, or other pet)
2. Why do you think Ben is sad? (He cannot find Rags.)

To answer an applied comprehension question the reader must extract the stated and implied information, compare and contrast it to his/her general knowledge, and arrive at a logical conclusion. To answer question number one, it is necessary to understand that: the name "Rags" is embossed on the leash (stated information); Ben cares about Rags (implied information); and that leashes are used for walking pets (general knowledge). To answer question number two, it is necessary to understand that: Ben had been looking for something (stated information); he could not find what he was looking for (implied information); Rags is probably what is missing (implied); and lost pets often make children sad (general knowledge).

Judgmental

Judgmental comprehension is the level at which the reader can process the information to arrive at an opinion or prediction that can be justified or supported with facts. For example:

1. What else might Ben do to find Rags?

To answer a judgmental comprehension question the reader must form an opinion or prediction that is logical to the story. There may be many acceptable answers, but they must be supported by the facts from the story and/or real life situations. For example, a child may answer, "I would put up posters of Rags with my phone number. That is what my friend did when she lost her dog. Ben wants to find Rags and the neighbors might be able to help."

Test Taking Tips

True and False

- Read the question carefully. If any part is false, mark the answer false.
- Look for key words like the words listed below. Think about what the words mean.

always	only	never	all
usually	every	frequently	often

Multiple Choice

- Read the question carefully. See if you know the answer <u>before</u> you look at the choices.
- Read <u>all</u> the choices, even if the first choice seems right.
- If you don't know which answer is correct, cross out the answers you know are <u>wrong</u>. Then, pick from the choices that are left.
- Always put down an answer. If you leave it blank, you know it is wrong. A guess might be right!

Matching

- Match the answers you know first.
- When you've made a match, cross out the number so you know it has been used.
- If you aren't sure, guess!

Ready-To-Use Ideas and Activities

The activities in this book will help children master the basic skills necessary to become competent test takers. Remember, as you read through the activities listed below, and as you go through this book, that all children learn at their own rate. Although repetition is important, it is critical that we never lose sight of the fact that it is equally important to build children's self-esteem and self-confidence if we want them to become successful learners.

Practice Test Taking

Reproduce the pages in this book to administer as a test to the students. Answers should be marked by completely darkening the "bubble" next to the selected choice. Practice tests may be administered in various ways: You may wish to select one practice sheet from each skill and give each student a "packet" similar to the standardized testing procedure. When the students are familiar with the practice test format, give them a practice timed test as most standardized tests are timed. It is suggested that three to five minutes be given for each page and that no test packet should exceed twenty minutes. You may also use the book as practice to reinforce particular skills.

Flash Cards

The back of this book has removable flash cards that will be great for use in basic skill and enrichment activities. Pull the flash cards out and cut them apart. If you have access to a paper cutter, use it to cut the flash cards apart. The following is just one of the ways you may want to use these flash cards.

Reproduce the bingo sheet on the next page in this book, making enough copies to have one for each student. Hand them out to the students. Take the flash cards and write the words on the chalk board. Have the students choose 24 of the words and write them in any order on the empty spaces of their bingo cards, writing only one word in each space. When all students have finished their cards, take the flash cards and make them into a deck. Call out the words one at a time. Any student who has a word that is called out should make an "X" through the word to cross it out. The first student who crosses out five words in a row (horizontally, vertically, or diagonally) wins the game. To extend the game, continue playing until a student crosses out all the words on his bingo sheet.

Vocabulary Bingo

		FREE		

Name ______________________________ Skill: Analogies

DIRECTIONS:
Read the statement and think about the relationships between the words. Then, read the answer choices. Mark the answer you have chosen.

1. LOUD is to THUNDER as LARGE is to

   a monkey
   b midget
   c whale
   d fly

2. TONE is to HEARING as COLOR is to

   f skin
   g sight
   h song
   j picture

3. CAT is to MOUSE as BIRD is to

   a worm
   b tail
   c cheese
   d hide

4. NOSE is to SMELL as TEETH is to

   f see
   g dentist
   h chew
   j toothpaste

5. WEAK is to STRONG as UNABLE is to

   a clumsy
   b coward
   c able
   d failure

6. PETAL is to FLOWER as FUR is to

   f coat
   g rabbit
   h warm
   j women

7. WEEK is to DAY as DAY is to

   a month
   b second
   c hour
   d night

8. CUP is to DRINK as PLATE is to

   f meal
   g dine
   h fork
   j silver

9. WATER is to BOAT as TRACK is to

   a search
   b runway
   c airplane
   d train

10. PLAYER is to TEAM as EAR is to

   f nose
   g body
   h foot
   j brain

Name ______________________________

Skill: Analogies

DIRECTIONS:
Read the statement and think about the relationships between the words. Then, read the answer choices. Mark the answer you have chosen.

1. EYE is to FACE as FINGER is to

   a toe
   b silver
   c hand
   d arm

2. SUMMER is to WINTER as EVENING is to

   f sunset
   g coolness
   h morning
   j darkness

3. WORDS is to BOOK as NOTES is to

   a piano
   b song
   c art
   d aroma

4. SKY is to GROUND as CEILING is to

   f plaster
   g roof
   h top
   j floor

5. CHALK is to BLACKBOARD as INK is to

   a pen
   b paper
   c desk
   d pencil

6. CALF is to COW as CUB is to

   f scout
   g bear
   h baby
   j woods

7. GRASS is to GREEN as SKY is to

   a star
   b blue
   c air
   d cloud

8. FATHER is to BROTHER as MOTHER is

   f daughter
   g sister
   h aunt
   j niece

9. FISH is to FINS as BIRD is to

   a fly
   b feather
   c wings
   d pigeon

10. RIGHT is to LEFT as LOW is to

   f bottom
   g high
   h sorrow
   j note

Name ______________________ Skill: Analogies

DIRECTIONS:
Read the statement and think about the relationships between the words. Then, read the answer choices. Mark the answer you have chosen.

1. ROSE is to RISE as WENT is to

   a going
   b gone
   c go
   d return

2. WATER is to AIR as BOAT is to

   f sail
   g sea
   h yacht
   j airplane

3. BARK is to DOG as ROAR is to

   a lion
   b snake
   c lamb
   d train

4. FIN is to FISH as PROPELLER is to

   f automobile
   g airplane
   h water
   j air

5. RING is to FINGER as SHOE is to

   a cobbler
   b lace
   c store
   d foot

6. TODAY is to YESTERDAY as PRESENT is to

   f yesterday
   g Monday
   h past
   j gift

7. LION is to CUB as MOTHER is to

   a aunt
   b child
   c father
   d grandmother

8. BLACK is to WHITE as NIGHT is to

   f stillness
   g sun
   h moon
   j day

9. ROOM is to HOUSE as TUB is to

   a kitchen
   b room
   c bathroom
   d building

10. ACT is to ACTRESS as SONG is to

    f songstress
    g singing
    h chorus
    j music

Name ______________________________

Skill: Analogies

DIRECTIONS:
Read the statement and think about the relationships between the words. Then, read the answer choices. Mark the answer you have chosen.

1. WALKS is to MAN as SWIMS is to

   a fish
   b pool
   c pier
   d boar

2. SCISSORS is to CUT as PEN is to

   f point
   g ink
   h pig
   j write

3. COLLAR is to NECK as BELT is to

   a body
   b buckle
   c waist
   d fastener

4. PLAY is to AUDIENCE as BOOK is to

   f writer
   g publisher
   h plot
   j reader

5. SKIN is to MAN as PELT is to

   a fish
   b fur
   c animal
   d scales

6. JOY is to SORROW as LAUGHTER is to

   f joke
   g fun
   h tears
   j ridicule

7. CALM is to STORM as PEACE is to

   a stillness
   b war
   c play
   d anger

8. SINKS is to ROCK as FLOATS is to

   f cork
   g light
   h flies
   j drowns

9. CAT is to MOUSE as WOLF is to

   a fox
   b sheep
   c dog
   d vulture

10. REFRIGERATOR is to MEAT as SAFE is to

    f teller
    g combination
    h money
    j watchman

Name ______________________

Skill: Analogies

DIRECTIONS:
Read the statement and think about the relationships between the words. Then, read the answer choices. Mark the answer you have chosen.

1. PEEL is to BANANA as SHELL is to

   a sea
   b fish
   c sand
   d oyster

2. FINGER is to HAND as HAIR is to

   f barber
   g baldness
   h scalp
   j blonde

3. FUR is to SQUIRREL as FEATHER is to

   a hat
   b tickle
   c light
   d bird

4. RAIN is to DROP as SNOW is to

   f ice
   g cold
   h zero
   j flake

5. ICE is to SKATE as WATER is to

   a swim
   b drink
   c rain
   d sport

6. WORST is to WORSE as WORSE is to

   f bad
   g good
   h best
   j better

7. BIRDS is to FEATHERS as FISH is to

   a fins
   b claws
   c gills
   d scales

8. PARACHUTE is to PLANE as LIFE PRESERVER is to

   f fish
   g boat
   h water
   j chest

9. HAND is to GLOVE as HEAD is to

   a hat
   b warmth
   c earmuffs
   d hair

10. TREE is to MAPLE as FLOWER is to

   f garden
   g hothouse
   h rose
   j shovel

Name ____________________

DIRECTIONS:
Read the statement and think about the relationships between the words. Then, read the answer choices. Mark the answer you have chosen.

1. STATION is to TRAIN as WHARF is to

   a ship
   b pier
   c water
   d river

2. TADPOLE is to FROG as CATERPILLAR is to

   f goose
   g butterfly
   h bird
   j flower

3. ACT is to PLAY as CHAPTER is to

   a page
   b book
   c library
   d title

4. CAPT. is to CAPTAIN as LB. is to

   f building
   g oz.
   h pound
   j ton

5. DECEMBER is to WINTER as JULY is to

   a spring
   b fall
   c autumn
   d summer

6. CAT is to FELINE as DOG is to

   f equine
   g wolf
   h canine
   j fangs

7. BED is to SLEEP as CHAIR is to

   a carry
   b sit
   c stare
   d awake

8. RIVER is to STREAM as MOUNTAIN is to

   f cliff
   g hill
   h canyon
   j valley

9. FEATHERS is to PLUCK as WOOL is to

   a sheep
   b weave
   c shear
   d comb

10. FLOWERS is to VASE as MILK is to

   f cow
   g udder
   h pitcher
   j farm

Name ______________________________ Skill: Analogies

DIRECTIONS:
Read the statement and think about the relationships between the words. Then, read the answer choices. Mark the answer you have chosen.

1. TONE is to DEAFNESS as COLOR is to

   a blindness
   b seeing
   c focus
   d darkness

2. TASTE is to TONGUE as TOUCH is to

   f finger
   g eye
   h feeling
   j borrow

3. TABLE is to CLOTH as BED is to

   a spread
   b mattress
   c pillow
   d ruffle

4. SNOW is to WINTER as RAIN is to

   f wet
   g summer
   h cold
   j flood

5. LID is to BOX as CORK is to

   a board
   b bottle
   c liquor
   d fire

6. THREE is to THIRD as ONE is to

   f fourth
   g last
   h second
   j first

7. CRIMINAL is to PRISON as PATIENT is to

   a illness
   b doctor
   c cure
   d hospital

8. GOOD is to BETTER as BAD is to

   f terrible
   g worse
   h improvement
   j worst

9. LADDER is to RUNG as STAIRWAY is to

   a building
   b floor
   c step
   d escalator

10. STILLNESS is to NOISE as DARKNESS is to

   f daylight
   g moonlight
   h night
   j twilight

Name ______________________________ Skill: Syllabication

DIRECTIONS:
In each question, the same word has been divided into syllables four different ways. Read the word to yourself and decide which answer is the correct way to divide the word. Mark the answer you have chosen.

1.
- **a** a-ccept-a-ble
- **b** ac-cep-ta-ble
- **c** ac-cept-a-ble
- **d** ac-cep-tab-le

2.
- **f** bew-il-der-ing
- **g** be-wil-der-ing
- **h** bew-il-der-ing
- **j** be-wild-er-ing

3.
- **a** e-mpha-size
- **b** em-phas-ize
- **c** em-pha-size
- **d** emp-has-ize

4.
- **f** me-rc-ury
- **g** mer-cur-y
- **h** mer-cu-ry
- **j** merc-u-ry

5.
- **a** se-mes-ter
- **b** sem-es-ter
- **c** se-mest-er
- **d** sem-est-er

6.
- **f** sup-er-vise
- **g** sup-erv-ise
- **h** su-perv-ise
- **j** su-per-vise

7.
- **a** al-ter-na-tive
- **b** alt-er-na-tive
- **c** al-tern-a-tive
- **d** alt-ern-a-tive

8.
- **f** co-mi-cal
- **g** com-i-cal
- **h** co-mic-al
- **j** com-ic-al

9.
- **a** im-pat-ience
- **b** imp-a-tience
- **c** im-pa-tience
- **d** imp-at-ience

10.
- **f** ob-ed-i-ence
- **g** o-be-di-ence
- **h** ob-ed-ie-nce
- **j** o-bed-i-ence

11.
- **a** sup-er-stit-ious
- **b** sup-ers-tit-ious
- **c** su-per-stit-ious
- **d** su-per-sti-tious

12.
- **f** rep-re-sen-ta-tion
- **g** rep-res-en-ta-tion
- **h** re-pres-ent-a-tion
- **j** rep-res-en-ta-tion

13.
- **a** aud-i-tion
- **b** a-ud-ition
- **c** a-udi-tion
- **d** au-di-tion

14.
- **f** con-tem-po-rar-y
- **g** con-temp-or-ar-y
- **h** cont-em-po-rar-y
- **j** cont-emp-or-ar-y

15.
- **a** int-er-vene
- **b** in-ter-vene
- **c** in-terv-ene
- **d** int-erv-ene

16.
- **f** pi-cco-lo
- **g** picc-o-lo
- **h** pic-co-lo
- **j** pic-col-o

17.
- **a** un-mis-ta-ka-ble
- **b** un-mis-tak-a-ble
- **c** un-mis-tak-ab-le
- **d** un-mi-stak-a-ble

18.
- **f** pa-ra-dise
- **g** pa-rad-ise
- **h** par-a-dise
- **j** par-ad-ise

Name ______________________________ Skill: Syllabication

DIRECTIONS:
In each question, the same word has been divided into syllables four different ways. Read the word to yourself and decide which answer is the correct way to divide the word. Mark the answer you have chosen.

1. **a** o-bje-ctive
   b obj-ec-tive
   c ob-jec-tive
   d ob-ject-ive

2. **f** det-er-gent
   g de-terg-ent
   h de-ter-gent
   j det-erg-ent

3. **a** aut-hen-tic
   b aut-hent-ic
   c au-then-tic
   d au-the-ntic

4. **f** imp-le-ment
   g im-ple-ment
   h imp-lem-ent
   j im-plem-ent

5. **a** par-lia-ment
   b parl-i-ament
   c par-liam-ent
   d parl-iam-ent

6. **f** un-pred-ict-a-ble
   g un-pred-ic-ta-ble
   h un-pre-dic-tab-le
   j un-pre-dict-a-ble

7. **a** ex-pect-a-tion
   b exp-ec-ta-tion
   c ex-pec-tat-ion
   d ex-pec-ta-tion

8. **f** char-ac-ter-is-tic
   g cha-rac-ter-ist-ic
   h char-act-er-is-tic
   j char-act-er-ist-ic

9. **a** cont-est-ant
   b con-tes-tant
   c con-test-ant
   d cont-es-tant

10. **f** in-tri-cate
    g int-ri-cate
    h in-tric-ate
    j int-ric-ate

11. **a** pin-nac-le
    b pi-nnac-le
    c pin-na-cle
    d pinn-a-cle

12. **f** surv-ey-or
    g sur-vey-or
    h surv-e-yor
    j sur-ve-yor

13. **a** em-phat-i-cal-ly
    b em-pha-ti-cal-ly
    c em-phat-i-call-y
    d em-pha-tic-al-ly

14. **f** am-end-ment
    g a-mend-ment
    h am-endm-ent
    j a-men-dment

15. **a** dra-ma-ti-call-y
    b dram-at-ic-al-ly
    c dram-a-ti-cal-ly
    d dra-mat-i-cal-ly

16. **f** o-blig-a-tion
    g o-blig-at-ion
    h ob-lig-a-tion
    j ob-li-ga-tion

17. **a** rep-rod-uce
    b re-pro-duce
    c rep-ro-duce
    d re-prod-uce

18. **f** sent-im-ent
    g sent-i-ment
    h sen-tim-ent
    j sen-ti-ment

Name ______________________________ Skill: Syllabication

DIRECTIONS:
In each question, the same word has been divided into syllables four different ways. Read the word to yourself and decide which answer is the correct way to divide the word. Mark the answer you have chosen.

1. **a** rep-rod-uc-tion
   b re-pro-duc-tion
   c rep-ro-duc-tion
   d re-prod-uc-tion

2. **f** me-tho-di-cal
   g meth-o-di-cal
   h meth-od-ic-al
   j me-thod-i-cal

3. **a** au-thor-i-ta-tive
   b au-tho-rit-a-tive
   c auth-o-rit-a-tive
   d auth-o-ri-ta-tive

4. **f** ac-com-plice
   g ac-comp-lice
   h acc-om-plice
   j acc-omp-lice

5. **a** di-al-ect
   b di-a-lect
   c di-ale-ct
   d dia-le-ct

6. **f** mult-i-pli-ca-tion
   g mul-ti-pli-ca-tion
   h mu-ltip-lic-a-tion
   j mult-ip-li-ca-tion

7. **a** part-ic-i-pate
   b part-i-ci-pate
   c par-tic-i-pate
   d par-ti-ci-pate

8. **f** in-va-lid
   g inv-ali-d
   h inv-a-lid
   j in-vali-d

9. **a** am-pli-fy
   b amp-li-fy
   c am-pl-ify
   d amp-lif-y

10. **f** ac-cord-i-on
    g acc-or-di-on
    h acc-ord-i-on
    j ac-cor-di-on

11. **a** her-o-ism
    b her-ois-m
    c he-ro-ism
    d he-roi-sm

12. **f** pa-rt-ition
    g part-i-tion
    h par-ti-tion
    j part-it-ion

13. **a** mul-ti-co-lored
    b mul-ti-col-ored
    c mu-lti-col-ored
    d mult-ic-ol-ored

14. **f** dia-go-na-l
    g di-ag-o-nal
    h di-a-gon-al
    j di-ag-on-al

15. **a** acc-or-ding-ly
    b acc-ord-ing-ly
    c ac-cord-ing-ly
    d ac-cor-ding-ly

16. **f** con-tra-dict
    g cont-ra-dict
    h con-trad-ict
    j cont-rad-ict

17. **a** inv-a-ri-ab-ly
    b in-va-ri-ab-ly
    c in-var-i-a-bly
    d in-va-ri-abl-y

18. **f** pr-ivac-y
    g priv-ac-y
    h pri-vac-y
    j pri-va-cy

Name ______________________ Skill: Syllabication

DIRECTIONS:
In each question, the same word has been divided into syllables four different ways. Read the word to yourself and decide which answer is the correct way to divide the word. Mark the answer you have chosen.

1. **a** re-quire-ment
   b req-uire-ment
   c re-quirem-ent
   d requ-irem-ent

2. **f** zoo-lo-gi-st
   g zo-ol-ogi-st
   h zo-ol-o-gist
   j zoo-log-is-t

3. **a** sy-mbo-lize
   b sym-bo-lize
   c sym-bol-ize
   d symb-ol-ize

4. **f** re-source-ful
   g re-sourcef-ul
   h res-ourc-eful
   j res-ource-ful

5. **a** pro-fit-ab-le
   b pro-fi-ta-ble
   c prof-it-a-ble
   d prof-i-ta-ble

6. **f** myth-o-log-y
   g my-thol-o-gy
   h my-tho-log-y
   j myth-o-lo-gy

7. **a** se-rio-us-ness
   b ser-i-ous-ness
   c se-ri-ou-sness
   d ser-io-us-ness

8. **f** un-su-spect-ing
   g un-su-spec-ting
   h un-sus-pect-ing
   j un-sus-pec-ting

9. **a** sta-tion-er-y
   b stat-i-on-ery
   c stat-ion-er-y
   d sta-tio-ner-y

10. **f** re-a-li-za-tion
    g re-al-iz-a-tion
    h re-al-iz-at-ion
    j re-al-i-za-tion

11. **a** prog-res-sive
    b pro-gres-sive
    c prog-ress-ive
    d pro-gress-ive

12. **f** nar-ra-tive
    g narr-a-tive
    h narr-at-ive
    j nar-rat-ive

13. **a** un-prot-ect-ed
    b un-pro-tec-ted
    c un-pro-tect-ed
    d un-prot-ect-ed

14. **f** un-an-im-ous
    g un-an-i-mous
    h u-nan-i-mous
    j u-na-ni-mous

15. **a** re-sid-ence
    b re-si-dence
    c res-id-ence
    d res-i-dence

16. **f** reb-el-lious
    g reb-ell-ious
    h re-bel-lious
    j re-bell-ious

17. **a** pa-tri-ot-ic
    b pat-ri-ot-ic
    c pa-tri-o-tic
    d pat-ri-ot-ic

18. **f** op-pos-it-ion
    g op-po-si-tion
    h op-pos-i-tion
    j op-po-sit-ion

Name ______________________________ Skill: Syllabication

DIRECTIONS:
In each question, the same word has been divided into syllables four different ways. Read the word to yourself and decide which answer is the correct way to divide the word. Mark the answer you have chosen.

1. **a** ma-gnes-ia
   b mag-ne-sia
   c mag-nes-ia
   d ma-gnes-ia

2. **f** le-ga-cy
   g le-gac-y
   h leg-ac-y
   j leg-a-cy

3. **a** in-du-stri-ous
   b in-dust-ri-ous
   c in-du-strio-us
   d in-dus-tri-ous

4. **f** ho-mesi-ckness
   g home-sic-kness
   h home-sick-ness
   j home-sickn-ess

5. **a** gla-mor-ous
   b gla-mo-rous
   c glam-o-rous
   d glam-or-ous

6. **f** ger-a-niu-m
   g ge-ra-ni-um
   h ger-a-ni-um
   j ge-ran-i-um

7. **a** main-te-nance
   b ma-inten-ance
   c main-ten-ance
   d main-tenan-ce

8. **f** ind-ig-na-tion
   g in-di-gna-tion
   h in-dig-na-tion
   j in-dig-nat-ion

9. **a** jav-e-lin
   b ja-vel-in
   c jav-el-in
   d ja-ve-lin

10. **f** hon-e-ymoon
    g ho-ney-moon
    h hon-eymo-on
    j hon-ey-moon

11. **a** ge-og-rap-hic-al
    b ge-o-graph-i-cal
    c ge-o-grap-hi-cal
    d ge-o-graph-ic-al

12. **f** fell-ow-ship
    g fel-low-ship
    h fell-o-wship
    j fel-lows-hip

13. **a** lea-der-ship
    b lea-ders-hip
    c lead-er-ship
    d lead-ers-hip

14. **f** ind-est-ruc-tib-le
    g in-de-struct-i-ble
    h in-des-truc-ti-ble
    j in-de-struc-tib-le

15. **a** le-gis-la-ture
    b leg-is-lat-ure
    c leg-is-la-ture
    d le-gi-slat-ure

16. **f** hos-til-i-ty
    g hos-ti-lit-y
    h host-il-i-ty
    j host-il-it-y

17. **a** gen-er-at-or
    b gen-er-a-tor
    c ge-ner-a-tor
    d ge-ne-ra-tor

18. **f** horr-i-fy-ing
    g horr-if-yi-ng
    h hor-rif-y-ing
    j hor-ri-fy-ing

Name ______________________________ Skill: Syllabication

DIRECTIONS:
In each question, the same word has been divided into syllables four different ways. Read the word to yourself and decide which answer is the correct way to divide the word. Mark the answer you have chosen.

1. **a** env-ir-on-ment-al
   b env-i-ron-men-tal
   c en-vir-on-ment-al
   d en-vi-ron-men-tal

2. **f** en-chant-ress
   g ench-ant-ress
   h enc-hant-ress
   j en-chan-tress

3. **a** ec-stat-ic
   b ec-sta-tic
   c ecs-ta-tic
   d ecs-tat-ic

4. **f** de-fen-seless
   g de-fense-less
   h def-en-seless
   j def-ense-less

5. **a** cord-u-roy
   b cor-du-roy
   c cord-ur-oy
   d cor-duro-y

6. **f** comp-u-tat-ion
   g comp-ut-a-tion
   h com-pu-ta-tion
   j com-put-a-tion

7. **a** en-thus-i-ast-ic
   b en-thu-si-as-tic
   c en-thus-i-as-tic
   d en-thu-si-ast-ic

8. **f** dum-bfoun-ded
   g dumb-foun-ded
   h dumb-found-ed
   j dum-bfound-ed

9. **a** dis-ap-pro-val
   b dis-ap-prov-al
   c di-sap-pro-val
   d di-sap-prov-al

10. **f** def-ian-ce
    g def-i-ance
    h de-fian-ce
    j de-fi-ance

11. **a** cos-met-ics
    b cos-me-tics
    c co-sme-tics
    d co-smet-ics

12. **f** cir-cu-la-tion
    g ci-rcul-at-ion
    h cir-cul-at-ion
    j circ-u-la-tion

13. **a** e-qui-va-lent
    b e-qui-val-ent
    c e-quiv-a-lent
    d e-quiv-al-ent

14. **f** e-con-o-mic
    g ec-o-no-mic
    h ec-on-om-ic
    j e-co-no-mic

15. **a** di-plo-mat
    b di-plom-at
    c dip-lo-mat
    d dip-lom-at

16. **f** cor-resp-ond-ence
    g cor-re-spond-ence
    h corr-e-spond-ence
    j cor-resp-on-dence

17. **a** del-ir-io-us
    b del-i-ri-ous
    c de-li-rio-us
    d de-lir-i-ous

18. **f** cam-ou-flage
    g cam-ouf-lage
    h ca-mou-flage
    j ca-moufl-age

Name ______________________________ Skill: Syllabication

DIRECTIONS:
In each question, the same word has been divided into syllables four different ways. Read the word to yourself and decide which answer is the correct way to divide the word. Mark the answer you have chosen.

1. **a** an-tis-ep-tic
b an-ti-sep-tic
c ant-i-sep-tic
d ant-is-ept-ic

2. **f** a-dol-es-cence
g a-do-lesc-ence
h ad-o-les-cence
j ad-ol-esc-ence

3. **a** cons-e-quent-ly
b cons-equ-en-tly
c con-seq-uen-tly
d con-se-quent-ly

4. **f** fund-am-en-tal
g fund-a-ment-al
h fun-dam-en-tal
j fun-da-men-tal

5. **a** in-sep-a-ra-ble
b in-se-par-ab-le
c ins-e-par-ab-le
d in-sepa-ra-b-le

6. **f** phi-los-o-pher
g phi-lo-sop-her
h phil-o-so-pher
j phil-o-sop-her

7. **a** at-mos-phe-ric
b at-mo-spher-ic
c at-mosp-he-ric
d at-mosp-her-ic

8. **f** ac-a-dem-ic
g ac-ad-e-mic
h ac-a-de-mic
j ac-ad-em-ic

9. **a** con-scien-tio-us
b con-sci-en-tious
c cons-ci-en-tious
d cons-ci-entio-us

10. **f** he-misp-here
g he-mis-phere
h hem-isp-here
j hem-i-sphere

11. **a** long-i-tude
b long-it-ude
c lon-gi-tude
d lon-git-ude

12. **f** ques-tion-abl-e
g ques-tion-a-ble
h quest-io-na-ble
j quest-ion-a-ble

13. **a** ag-ric-ul-tu-ral
b ag-ri-cul-tur-al
c ag-ric-ult-u-ral
d ag-ri-cult-ur-al

14. **f** bel-iev-ab-le
g bel-iev-a-ble
h be-liev-ab-le
j be-liev-a-ble

15. **a** dom-est-ic-ate
b dom-es-ti-cate
c do-mes-ti-cate
d do-mest-ic-ate

16. **f** im-ag-i-na-ble
g im-a-gin-a-ble
h i-mag-i-na-ble
j i-ma-gin-ab-le

17. **a** mom-en-tar-y
b mom-ent-a-ry
c mo-men-tar-y
d mo-ment-a-ry

18. **f** ter-mi-na-tion
g ter-min-a-tion
h term-i-na-tion
j term-in-a-tion

Name ________________________________ Skill: Spelling

DIRECTIONS:
Look at each group of words. Decide which word in each group is not spelled correctly. Mark the answer you have chosen.

1. **a** abdomen **b** brink **c** applesause **d** charity
2. **f** strangle **g** teerful **h** tiresome **j** undecided
3. **a** raid **b** pave **c** repeetedly **d** rafter
4. **f** destinashion **g** conceal **h** chemist **j** bronco
5. **a** destined **b** drowsy **c** era **d** fevirish
6. **f** savor **g** sinnester **h** specialize **j** streetlight
7. **a** equator **b** foster **c** greenhouse **d** jellifish
8. **f** withdraw **g** verb **h** undersea **j** teknical
9. **a** popularety **b** offerings **c** jest **d** incline
10. **f** appoint **g** abdomen **h** abide **j** apreciation
11. **a** griddel **b** holder **c** increasing **d** jiggle
12. **f** tollbooth **g** unearth **h** vertikal **j** workable
13. **a** litirature **b** mental **c** offense **d** silversmith
14. **f** strategy **g** similarity **h** savings **j** republick
15. **a** greenish **b** forteenth **c** festivity **d** drizzle
16. **f** barrier **g** browse **h** cherish **j** kritter
17. **a** loan **b** merciful **c** peecock **d** rainwater
18. **f** workmen **g** uneven **h** tombe **j** strengthen

Name ______________________________ Skill: Spelling

DIRECTIONS:
Look at each group of words. Decide which word in each group is not spelled correctly. Mark the answer you have chosen.

1. **a** species **b** sawdust **c** rescque **d** ramble

2. **f** destiny **g** brute **h** appropriate **j** abssence

3. **a** grinder **b** honeycombe **c** indifferent **d** jab

4. **f** stroller **g** torment **h** unfassen **j** vex

5. **a** penetrate **b** navigatter **c** locust **d** inexperience

6. **f** arbor **g** acuse **h** bathrobe **j** burglar

7. **a** portray **b** jubilent **c** homestead **d** grill

8. **f** abstract **g** concussion **h** crossroad **j** destroiyer

9. **a** locomotive **b** naval **c** possture **d** rank

10. **f** vibbrate **g** unfinished **h** torpedo **j** submarine

11. **a** honorary **b** guarantee **c** fiesta **d** eskort

12. **f** conferm **g** crutch **h** diaper **j** essay

13. **a** fragranse **b** fiction **c** erase **d** drummer

14. **f** duet **g** erupt **h** figget **j** freshness

15. **a** resentmint **b** sayings **c** sissy **d** spectator

16. **f** teeter **g** skab **h** resistance **j** rapture

17. **a** dwellings **b** crummy **c** confide **d** civalized

18. **f** finance **g** frightfull **h** hopper **j** infant

Name ______________________________ Skill: Spelling

DIRECTIONS:
Look at each group of words. Decide which word in each group is <u>not</u> spelled correctly. Mark the answer you have chosen.

1. **a** keg
   b logbook
   c middair
   d perfume

2. **f** worship
   g violinist
   h unhook
   j temporery

3. **a** necktar
   b kennel
   c horrid
   d habitat

4. **f** acheive
   g arise
   h burner
   j connection

5. **a** subburb
   b tragic
   c identified
   d visor

6. **f** eturnal
   g rave
   h host
   j curse

7. **a** powerless
   b rascal
   c skalp
   d spicy

8. **f** spiderweb
   g skateboard
   h schoolbook
   j resourse

9. **a** frustrat
   b fingernail
   c differ
   d cue

10. **f** digest
    g establish
    h inherit
    j keeboard

11. **a** worthwhile
    b vital
    c unlach
    d tenderness

12. **f** clamp
    g burnt
    h acquire
    j beecon

13. **a** submitt
    b torture
    c violence
    d worrisome

14. **f** raspping
    g prank
    h persist
    j oppose

15. **a** confound
    b clammy
    c burlap
    d battelfield

16. **f** needless
    g oral
    h precaution
    j restraine

17. **a** spire
    b skiper
    c scorch
    d retold

18. **f** earfones
    g firsthand
    h fund
    j hostile

Name ______________________________ Skill: Spelling

DIRECTIONS:
Look at each group of words. Decide which word in each group is <u>not</u> spelled correctly. Mark the answer you have chosen.

1. **a** injustice
   b kin
   c migrashun
   d nervous

2. **f** vocabulary
   g funnle
   h unnatural
   j splatter

3. **a** consarvation
   b aspect
   c administration
   d bedspread

4. **f** flannel
   g clense
   h furrow
   j inscription

5. **a** spongy
   b sunbeam
   c text
   d tribut

6. **f** secretive
   g revive
   h outcome
   j neice

7. **a** ordeal
   b fantom
   c prefix
   d slain

8. **f** raven
   g nestle
   h lowers
   j bushle

9. **a** admmission
   b buttermilk
   c considerable
   d leave

10. **f** knobby
    g lull
    h miniature
    j eternaty

11. **a** unpainted
    b voter
    c writings
    d vowle

12. **f** minimum
    g lunar
    h knotwhole
    j insight

13. **a** splendor
    b unmoving
    c vitiman
    d wreath

14. **f** knack
    g bearskin
    h clash
    j custumary

15. **a** cyclone
    b discouragement
    c asortment
    d evaporate

16. **f** originate
    g principel
    h reality
    j sleet

17. **a** unplesant
    b sunburn
    c sponsor
    d sleigh

18. **f** housework
    g fuse
    h examinashun
    j flashbulb

Name ______________________ Skill: Spelling

DIRECTIONS:
Look at each group of words. Decide which word in each group is <u>not</u> spelled correctly. Mark the answer you have chosen.

1. **a** disgusted
   b dainty
   c construct
   d candedate

2. **f** flimesy
   g gait
   h halter
   j hover

3. **a** spotless
   b thieft
   c trigger
   d unreasonable

4. **f** proceedure
   g outsider
   h noodle
   j misfortune

5. **a** affectionate
   b attractive
   c biology
   d cappable

6. **f** missile
   g noose
   h riggid
   j squish

7. **a** attentive
   b atitude
   c canteen
   d contentment

8. **f** insisstent
   g knuckle
   h mink
   j nitrogen

9. **a** wad
   b yeild
   c wage
   d unsafe

10. **f** lank
    g instrucktor
    h humanity
    j garment

11. **a** clunk
    b contrary
    c darn
    d dissmal

12. **f** thickness
    g unssucessful
    h wallet
    j zest

13. **a** dampness
    b effecktive
    c dishwasher
    d exceeding

14. **f** probbable
    g rearrange
    h sector
    j sling

15. **a** triple
    b sprig
    c richnes
    d squad

16. **f** exception
    g continual
    h binnocular
    j attorney

17. **a** effortless
    b insurrance
    c fluster
    d hasty

18. **f** wanderer
    g untidy
    h tropical
    j survivver

Name ________________________ Skill: Spelling

DIRECTIONS:
Look at each group of words. Decide which word in each group is not spelled correctly. Mark the answer you have chosen.

1. **a** starfish **b** riot **c** propportion **d** recheck

2. **f** bleech **g** audio **h** aimless **j** cardinal

3. **a** pinto **b** prosper **c** recognize **d** robbary

4. **f** unused **g** sustain **h** swager **j** snakebite

5. **a** ideal **b** headings **c** geology **d** zooloogy

6. **f** alein **g** awesome **h** core **j** corncob

7. **a** misunderstood **b** maddness **c** humiliate **d** foal

8. **f** convert **g** dispose **h** eleveneth **j** hazy

9. **a** session **b** smeer **c** suspend **d** thirty-six

10. **f** shanty **g** rockker **h** recount **j** protect

11. **a** foklore **b** expense **c** employ **d** division

12. **f** dejected **g** dizzyness **h** explosive **j** fondness

13. **a** hazzard **b** dispatch **c** deafen **d** contribute

14. **f** hustle **g** lavender **h** noticable **j** overcame

15. **a** troublemaker **b** untouched **c** zookeeper **d** wanderor

16. **f** pichfork **g** placement **h** overcast **j** nourish

17. **a** coldness **b** deffensive **c** carvings **d** bloodhound

18. **f** identification **g** leese **h** overgrown **j** rotate

Name ____________________ Skill: Spelling

DIRECTIONS:
Look at each group of words. Decide which word in each group is not spelled correctly. Mark the answer you have chosen.

1. **a** snuze **b** static **c** sweeper **d** snowfall
2. **f** nylon **g** nucleer **h** monitor **j** management
3. **a** glaze **b** extension **c** document **d** delliberate
4. **f** coresspond **g** delighted **h** encircle **j** factor
5. **a** historic **b** heater **c** immortal **d** ilegal
6. **f** mathematics **g** meek **h** margin **j** mannual
7. **a** uproot **b** warlike **c** twang **d** truse
8. **f** lejendary **g** invade **h** idol **j** igloo
9. **a** collide **b** babboon **c** camouflage **d** alternate
10. **f** encownter **g** engage **h** forecast **j** foghorn
11. **a** islander **b** issolate **c** jailer **d** janitor
12. **f** objection **g** oatmeal **h** obbstacle **j** occupant
13. **a** steadfast **b** snowman **c** sheepish **d** rectanggle
14. **f** heartbroken **g** gleaful **h** forearm **j** foothold
15. **a** altitude **b** amber **c** blueish **d** colorless
16. **f** glimmer **g** grammer **h** hesitant **j** hideout
17. **a** literachure **b** likewise **c** limestone **d** listing
18. **f** reject **g** reluctant **h** remmedy **j** remainder

Name ______________________________ Skill: Synonyms

DIRECTIONS:
Read each sentence and the underlined choices. Select the answer that means about the same thing as the underlined word or words. Mark the answer you have chosen.

1. Is this an <u>acceptable</u> answer to your question?
   - **a** hinder
   - **b** bad
   - **c** alright
   - **d** perplexing

2. I <u>beseech</u> you to do your best on the test because it is important to your grade.
   - **f** tell
   - **g** beg
   - **h** demand
   - **j** command

3. The crowd was in a <u>furor</u> when their team won.
   - **a** upset
   - **b** uproar
   - **c** arguing
   - **d** happy

4. There is just one <u>flaw</u> in your plan.
   - **f** blemish
   - **g** point
   - **h** drawing
   - **j** moment

5. The dance was <u>memorable</u> for everyone.
   - **a** notable
   - **b** forgettable
   - **c** fun
   - **d** awful

6. The boy wrinkled his brow in <u>consternation</u> at the puzzling question.
   - **f** excitement
   - **g** anger
   - **h** arching
   - **j** dismay

7. Put more <u>emphasis</u> on that line in the play.
   - **a** stress
   - **b** laughter
   - **c** detail
   - **d** movement

8. <u>Immobilize</u> the broken arm before the boy tries to move.
   - **f** bandage
   - **g** heal
   - **h** make motionless
   - **j** help

9. Carl has been a <u>laborer</u> all his life.
   - **a** man
   - **b** president
   - **c** counselor
   - **d** worker

10. Meet me at the <u>intersection</u> of Maple and Elm.
   - **f** street
   - **g** corner
   - **h** lane
   - **j** side

Name ______________________________ Skill: Synonyms

DIRECTIONS:
Read each sentence and the underlined choices. Select the answer that means about the same thing as the underlined word or words. Mark the answer you have chosen.

1. Can you come to the dance recital with me?
   - **a** stage
   - **b** party
   - **c** display
   - **d** show

2. I will repay the money next Tuesday.
   - **f** borrow
   - **g** loan
   - **h** take back
   - **j** pay back

3. Cook the pancakes in the hot skillet.
   - **a** oven
   - **b** sun
   - **c** pan
   - **d** fire

4. The sky was sunless when the dark clouds drifted across it.
   - **f** bright
   - **g** hollow
   - **h** cloudy
   - **j** smaller

5. Will John testify at the trial?
   - **a** tattle
   - **b** give evidence
   - **c** stand up
   - **d** advise

6. Joe was in a precarious position when he stood on the chair with the loose leg!
   - **f** tall
   - **g** laughable
   - **h** dangerous
   - **j** irresistible

7. Peggy always shuns work she doesn't like.
   - **a** finishes
   - **b** ignores
   - **c** handles
   - **d** holds

8. We collected a sizable amount of money for the charity.
   - **f** large
   - **g** small
   - **h** modest
   - **j** humble

9. We have an unlimited supply of towels for the pool party.
   - **a** minor
   - **b** unending
   - **c** definite
   - **d** absolute

10. Susan has a lot of vitality even though she is eighty years old.
    - **f** happiness
    - **g** wrinkles
    - **h** energy
    - **j** wisdom

Name ______________________________ Skill: Synonyms

DIRECTIONS:
Read each sentence and the underlined choices. Select the answer that means about the same thing as the underlined word or words. Mark the answer you have chosen.

1. I left my car in the vicinity of that flag pole.
   - **a** parking lot
   - **b** under
   - **c** area
   - **d** shadow

2. The hunters went into the woodland to find a fox.
   - **f** pasture
   - **g** farm
   - **h** forest
   - **j** desert

3. The trio sang a lovely harmony.
   - **a** two
   - **b** duet
   - **c** three
   - **d** pair

4. That cut on your hand should not be submerged in the dish water.
   - **f** damp
   - **g** floating
   - **h** put under
   - **j** heated

5. The corn field looks sparse because the heavy rains ruined many plants.
   - **a** muddy
   - **b** bare
   - **c** quiet
   - **d** elated

6. This face cream is supposed to give you a youthful look!
   - **f** babyish
   - **g** old
   - **h** young
   - **j** radiant

7. The birds began to trill as the sun rose in the sky.
   - **a** sing
   - **b** rouse
   - **c** take flight
   - **d** hide

8. Did you subscribe to that magazine?
   - **f** write
   - **g** read
   - **h** order
   - **j** sell

9. The scientist speculated about life on other planets.
   - **a** denied
   - **b** refused
   - **c** enjoyed
   - **d** thought

10. I had a spasm in my foot when my muscles cramped.
   - **f** contraction
   - **g** splinter
   - **h** warmth
   - **j** tiredness

Name ______________________________ Skill: Synonyms

DIRECTIONS:
Read each sentence and the underlined choices. Select the answer that means about the same thing as the underlined word or words. Mark the answer you have chosen.

1. Bobby went on vacation to get a little <u>relaxation</u>.
   - **a** tan
   - **b** rest
   - **c** slumber
   - **d** money

2. The librarian told the noisy boy to <u>shush</u>.
   - **f** leave
   - **g** run
   - **h** respect
   - **j** quiet down

3. During the storm at sea, water was coming in through the <u>portholes</u> of the ship.
   - **a** cracks
   - **b** windows
   - **c** stern
   - **d** floor

4. The twins looked <u>identical</u>!
   - **f** cute
   - **g** older
   - **h** alike
   - **j** alive

5. The land was fertile and ready for planting.
   - **a** dried up
   - **b** rich
   - **c** dusty
   - **d** damp

6. Do not <u>scald</u> yourself in the hot shower!
   - **f** wet
   - **g** steam
   - **h** burn
   - **j** dry

7. The little boy had <u>puny</u> muscles and could not lift the heavy books.
   - **a** hefty
   - **b** weak
   - **c** large
   - **d** developed

8. Please <u>mince</u> the onions for the soup.
   - **f** eat
   - **g** wash
   - **h** finely chop
   - **j** cook

9. We <u>frequently</u> have homework because the teachers think it is important.
   - **a** never
   - **b** always
   - **c** sometimes
   - **d** often

10. The teacher will <u>evaluate</u> the projects and tell us our grades.
    - **f** review
    - **g** pass over
    - **h** rate
    - **j** deliver

Name ______________________________ Skill: Synonyms

DIRECTIONS:
Read each sentence and the underlined choices. Select the answer that means about the same thing as the underlined word or words. Mark the answer you have chosen.

1. I cannot disclose any information about the accident until the police come.
   - **a** reveal
   - **b** hide
   - **c** receive
   - **d** find

2. Jeff and Bob had a conflict over which television show they would watch.
   - **f** agreement
   - **g** disagreement
   - **h** discussion
   - **j** alignment

3. The edge of the knife was rather blunt from years of use.
   - **a** sharp
   - **b** notched
   - **c** wavy
   - **d** dull

4. The water became frigid after the first snow of the season.
   - **f** quiet
   - **g** roiled
   - **h** icy
   - **j** warmer

5. Billy and Fred have been chums since first grade.
   - **a** pals
   - **b** enemies
   - **c** neighbors
   - **d** strangers

6. Howard dwelt with the nomads for three years.
   - **f** ate
   - **g** danced
   - **h** lived
   - **j** hurried

7. The bird would mimic everything the pirate said.
   - **a** deny
   - **b** outlaw
   - **c** repeat
   - **d** sing

8. The desolate land had not been farmed in many years.
   - **f** barren
   - **g** rocky
   - **h** enormous
   - **j** logical

9. The exterior of the house looked neglected, but the inside was freshly remodeled.
   - **a** back
   - **b** basement
   - **c** porch
   - **d** outside

10. The baby birds became boisterous when they were hungry.
   - **f** featherless
   - **g** noisy
   - **h** quiet
   - **j** tender

Name ______________________

DIRECTIONS:
Read each sentence and the underlined choices. Select the answer that means about the same thing as the underlined word or words. Mark the answer you have chosen.

1. The hikers began their ascent up the mountain path.
   - **a** decline
   - **b** rise
   - **c** jog
   - **d** deception

2. It was futile to dial the phone when the wires had been cut.
   - **f** dangerous
   - **g** outrageous
   - **h** helpful
   - **j** useless

3. The historian was excavating the field where some children found an arrowhead.
   - **a** covering
   - **b** protecting
   - **c** digging
   - **d** selling

4. The knolls across the land made it impossible to see very far.
   - **f** trees
   - **g** hills
   - **h** people
   - **j** houses

5. The king was overthrown and exiled to a small island.
   - **a** confiscated
   - **b** crowned
   - **c** banned
   - **d** insulated

6. The brooch looked like a star covered with diamonds.
   - **f** spotlight
   - **g** recital
   - **h** pin
   - **j** hat

7. It is hard to domesticate some types of birds.
   - **a** capture
   - **b** tame
   - **c** raise
   - **d** photograph

8. The sheep's fleece was dyed and made into cloth.
   - **f** wool
   - **g** feathers
   - **h** silk
   - **j** nylon

9. James is ignorant of the rules in this classroom.
   - **a** imposing
   - **b** unaware
   - **c** understanding
   - **d** breaking

10. The clown was clad in huge shoes, baggy pants, and a pink wig.
    - **f** dressed
    - **g** disguised
    - **h** identified
    - **j** playing

Name ____________________ Skill: Synonyms

DIRECTIONS:
Read each sentence and the underlined choices. Select the answer that means about the same thing as the underlined word or words. Mark the answer you have chosen.

1. Jason loathes doing so much homework every evening.
   - **a** despises
   - **b** enjoys
   - **c** requires
   - **d** remembers

2. The thief's motive for stealing the bread was that he had not eaten in three days.
   - **f** statement
   - **g** need
   - **h** reason
   - **j** scheme

3. Judy retained the ticket stub from the concert to put in her scrapbook.
   - **a** ejected
   - **b** omitted
   - **c** hid
   - **d** kept

4. The class shouted, "Yes!" in unison when the teacher asked if they were ready to go.
   - **f** apart
   - **g** as one
   - **h** loudly
   - **j** quietly

5. There is nothing more to say so the meeting is now terminated.
   - **a** enlisted
   - **b** engaged
   - **c** revered
   - **d** ended

6. The bird's plumage was bright and colorful.
   - **f** beak
   - **g** flight
   - **h** feathers
   - **j** family

7. The hikers were excited when they reached the summit of the mountain!
   - **a** bottom
   - **b** middle
   - **c** rocky side
   - **d** top

8. Randy used his hatchet to sever the branch from the tree.
   - **f** bend
   - **g** cut
   - **h** capsize
   - **j** hang

9. I have a tendency to buy new shoes when I go shopping.
   - **a** inclination
   - **b** disposition
   - **c** desire
   - **d** restriction

10. The soldier used his saber to cut his way through the dense bushes.
    - **f** explosives
    - **g** laser
    - **h** sword
    - **j** horse

Name ______________________________ Skill: Homophones

DIRECTIONS:
Read each group of phrases. One of the underlined words is not spelled correctly for the way it is used in the sentence. Mark the word that is not spelled correctly.

1. **a** she was so rude
   b bale out the boat
   c patients needed a doctor
   d the air pressure is low

2. **f** this puzzle is a maze
   g a deep red wine
   h flew through the air
   j colonel of popcorn

3. **a** she has the write address
   b such a rude person
   c a bluish hue to it
   d my patience is wearing thin

4. **f** brothers love to tease
   g rued little boy
   h mourn the death of a pet
   j papers got wet

5. **a** don't teas the puppy
   b hew the limb from the tree
   c don't whine at me
   d have patience with the project

6. **f** shake with your right hand
   g Indians ate maize
   h bale of hay
   j a wine from the violin strings

7. **a** children tease each other
   b grind the maze into flour
   c rued the mistake
   d dye it a new hue of purple

8. **f** we will morn her absence
   g write a report
   h bail the water
   j maize is grown in Mexico

9. **a** we mourn the loss
   b puppy will whine
   c a wet day
   d patients is a virtue

10. **f** face had a red hue
    g whet after the rain
    h bail water from the boat
    j heir got all the money

Name ______________________________ Skill: Homophones

DIRECTIONS:
Read each group of phrases. One of the underlined words is not spelled correctly for the way it is used in the sentence. Mark the word that is not spelled correctly.

1. **a** right a thank-you note to grandmother
   b a rude remark
   c he will write the program
   d out of jail on bail

2. **f** the lady brews the tea
   g took her eye off the ball
   h an ornate earn
   j the cleaning crews came later

3. **a** we will leave next week
   b he bruise the tea
   c ducked out of the rain
   d punch a hole with the awl

4. **f** duct into the tunnel
   g voted aye or nay
   h a big purple bruise
   j loot from the party

5. **a** pirate's lute was buried
   b the steaming brews
   c one weak until the holiday
   d jeans are allowed here

6. **f** air duct was blocked
   g play the lute
   h not aloud to go with you
   j rein in the horse

7. **a** awl these years
   b I am here
   c he earns a lot of money
   d rain all day long

8. **f** a wedding rite
   g urn a lot of money
   h take a cruise to Spain
   j a song in F minor

9. **a** large urn in the garden
   b weak with hunger
   c read aloud to children
   d it rained all weak

10. **f** miner mistake on the paper
    g a cruise ship
    h reign over the country
    j a lot of loot in the store

Name ____________________ Skill: Homophones

DIRECTIONS:
Read each group of phrases. One of the underlined words is not spelled correctly for the way it is used in the sentence. Mark the word that is <u>not</u> spelled correctly.

1.
- **a** we <u>all</u> heard it
- **b** working with <u>crews</u> of men
- **c** king will <u>rein</u> over us
- **d** <u>write</u> the essay

2.
- **f** my <u>write</u> foot
- **g** not <u>allowed</u> to go
- **h** see with the <u>eye</u>
- **j** played in the <u>minor</u> league

3.
- **a** sang an <u>ode</u> to the school
- **b** she <u>taught</u> school
- **c** the <u>ail</u> tasted bitter
- **d** worn out old <u>shoe</u>

4.
- **f** go <u>chute</u> at the targets
- **g** a <u>shoe</u> with laces
- **h** he <u>taught</u> me well
- **j** likes <u>soul</u> music

5.
- **a** a corn <u>bin</u> in the barn
- **b** pull <u>aweigh</u> from the curb
- **c** a <u>doe</u> and her fawn
- **d** cord is stretched <u>taut</u>

6.
- **f** <u>all</u> of us are going
- **g** <u>ducked</u> and it missed me
- **h** turn <u>right</u> at the corner
- **j** got hit in the <u>aye</u>

7.
- **a** <u>earn</u> his respect
- **b** <u>crews</u> the ocean on a ship
- **c** a coal <u>miner</u>
- **d** a storm <u>brews</u> out west

8.
- **f** one <u>per</u> customer
- **g** <u>shoot</u> the gun
- **h** a <u>been</u> for potatoes
- **j** the horse's <u>mane</u>

9.
- **a** health began to <u>ail</u>
- **b** <u>lie</u> down to rest
- **c** earned a lot of <u>dough</u>
- **d** the <u>mane</u> problem

10.
- **f** <u>owed</u> you a favor
- **g** were <u>away</u> for the day
- **h** use a white flour <u>doe</u> for bread
- **j** have <u>been</u> able to use it

Name ______________________ Skill: Homophones

DIRECTIONS:
Read each group of phrases. One of the underlined words is not spelled correctly for the way it is used in the sentence. Mark the word that is not spelled correctly.

1. **a** purr when it is happy
   b I've been to market
   c anchors aweigh
   d go lye on the bed

2. **f** drank ale in the pub
   g he ode lots of money
   h sole of the shoe
   j cat began to purr

3. **a** was the soul person in the room
   b shoot at the target
   c moved to Maine
   d lye used to make soap

4. **f** the ball was a success
   g a bow on the package
   h baring good news
   j it may rain tomorrow

5. **a** wore a yellow beau in her hair
   b the king enjoyed a long reign
   c dog was baring its teeth
   d throw the ball to me

6. **f** not a soul was there
   g shoe away the goats
   h the main artery
   j a coal chute in the basement

7. **a** don't tell a lie
   b fifty words purr minute
   c sang "do-re-me"
   d brewed the ale in huge vats

8. **f** had a taught look to her face
   g shoo away the flies
   h owed five dollars
   j going away tomorrow

9. **a** bearing gifts of joy
   b baby started to bawl
   c a pretty red bow
   d two inches of reign

10. **f** she will reign over the country
    g rolled sleeves baring his arms
    h went to the prince's bawl
    j the beau picked up his date

Name ______________________________ Skill: Homophones

DIRECTIONS:
Read each group of phrases. One of the underlined words is not spelled correctly for the way it is used in the sentence. Mark the word that is not spelled correctly.

1.
- **a** a bird coop
- **b** the drawing was a symbol
- **c** the banned played on
- **d** fish swam in the coral

2.
- **f** people crowded in the I'll
- **g** a tall beech tree
- **h** the seed grew
- **j** a small isle at sea

3.
- **a** tree is a cymbal of life
- **b** a nun lives in the convent
- **c** a green yew tree
- **d** band together for strength

4.
- **f** car was a two seated coupe
- **g** the enemy will soon cede
- **h** play the cymbal in the band
- **j** caste an eye at her

5.
- **a** I'll bake the cake
- **b** an apple cede
- **c** cast sand on the icy walk
- **d** went to the choral concert

6.
- **f** a sandy beach
- **g** found a starfish on the beech
- **h** how are you
- **j** none of us can go

7.
- **a** a symbol of excellence
- **b** a marching band
- **c** fox in the chicken coop
- **d** she has nun left

8.
- **f** seed the field
- **g** walked up the aisle
- **h** choral in the ocean
- **j** cast the net

9.
- **a** the yew had a lamb
- **b** a coral reef
- **c** the elite caste of India
- **d** we played at the beach

10.
- **f** the ewe and the ram
- **g** the boy hit the ball
- **h** dogs in the chicken coupe
- **j** the seed grew into a flower

Name ______________________________ Skill: Homophones

DIRECTIONS:
Read each group of phrases. One of the underlined words is not spelled correctly for the way it is used in the sentence. Mark the word that is not spelled correctly.

1.
a a golf coarse
b hoard the money
c a duel with swords
d laces through the eyelets

2.
f gorillas ate the bananas
g take a course at college
h Robin Hood and Fryer Tuck
j his temper flares up

3.
a a palm tree on the eyelet
b fire flared up then died
c the creek is dry
d a frank answer

4.
f a horde of ants
g a gilt comb and brush
h the wool felt coarse
j feelings of gilt

5.
a dual airbags
b the hinges creek
c the French have the franc
d gorillas at the zoo

6.
f my new shoes creak
g mirror with a gilt frame
h a skirt that flairs at the bottom
j the boy was franc and honest

7.
a shot flairs into the sky
b the friar at the church
c a horde of angry people
d guerrillas plotted against the army

8.
f let's be frank about this
g had duel tires on the car
h a small islet in the stream
j a deep fryer for doughnuts

9.
a the sixth eyelet on the shoe
b gorilla warriors retreated
c car had dual exhaust pipes
d a coarse file for nails

10.
f fish live in the creek
g sorry and full of guilt
h chicken was a perfect fryer
j hoard of bees flew from the nest

Name ____________________

Skill: Homophones

DIRECTIONS:
Read each group of phrases. One of the underlined words is not spelled correctly for the way it is used in the sentence. Mark the word that is not spelled correctly.

1.
- **a** don't sail in stormy whether
- **b** those are leaded glass windows
- **c** raise the window higher
- **d** docked at the pier

2.
- **f** a tier rolled down her cheek
- **g** the mall is having a great sale
- **h** we have rung the doorbell
- **j** use the oar in the boat

3.
- **a** push with all your might
- **b** a tear dropped from her cheek
- **c** I raze puppies for a living
- **d** the fresh scent of sizzling bacon

4.
- **f** he led the class in the pledge
- **g** peer into the window
- **h** whether or not you like it
- **j** choose either him ore me

5.
- **a** we might have a test today
- **b** she wrung her hands in worry
- **c** take me to the maul tomorrow
- **d** a few rays of the sun

6.
- **f** a tiny mite of a girl
- **g** top tier of the stadium
- **h** she rung the clothes after washing
- **j** we mined for iron ore

7.
- **a** write with a lead pencil
- **b** was sent to the grocery store
- **c** nasty weather in winter
- **d** we scent a message to you

8.
- **f** raze the building
- **g** a huge ship was at the peer
- **h** a wreck would maul the car
- **j** a rung on the ladder

9.
- **a** it mite rain tonight
- **b** he shed a tear or two
- **c** juice or milk for breakfast
- **d** he sent her some flowers

10.
- **f** shop at the mall
- **g** the weather is improving
- **h** she lead the band in the parade
- **j** they were peers at school

Name ______________________

Skill: Vocabulary

DIRECTIONS:
Read each sentence and the answer choices. Choose the word or phrase that best completes the sentence. Mark the answer you have chosen.

1. To try out for a part in a play is to

   a audition
   b nozzle
   c jockey
   d lounge

2. An irritating rub is

   f chafing
   g gouge
   h hackle
   j immobilize

3. To remove a piece is to

   a elate
   b correspond
   c detach
   d ignore

4. A wide unbroken stretch is an

   f recovery
   g vapor
   h velocity
   j expanse

5. Something done quickly and in secret is

   a listless
   b furtive
   c puny
   d quizzical

6. Something that is confusing is

   f bewildering
   g precarious
   h incorrect
   j distorted

7. Something that is funny is

   a comical
   b gruesome
   c fictional
   d forage

8. When you stress a word you

   f symbolize
   g emphasize
   h digest
   j ridicule

9. A young bird that has just grown feathers is a

   a riffle
   b fledgling
   c nomad
   d juggler

10. Something that is dirty or unclean is

   f industrial
   g marathon
   h grubby
   j fateful

Name ______________________________ Skill: Vocabulary

DIRECTIONS:
Read each sentence and the answer choices. Choose the word or phrase that best completes the sentence. Mark the answer you have chosen.

1. A word that means "as a result of" is

   a disclose
   b cope
   c hence
   d ignite

2. To step in or come between is to

   f agitate
   g agonize
   h intervene
   j complicate

3. When you take something for granted without proving it you

   a presume
   b overcrowd
   c negotiate
   d maroon

4. An exact copy of something is a

   f unison
   g tendon
   h replica
   j scribe

5. Half of one school year is a

   a semester
   b reviewer
   c noonday
   d kindergarten

6. A person who doesn't wait for anything is

   f dutiful
   g impatient
   h domestic
   j grievous

7. A small flute-like instrument is a

   a bandanna
   b portable
   c piccolo
   d inkling

8. Something that happens totally by chance happens at

   f random
   g mutiny
   h latitude
   j impractical

9. Having a fresh healthy red look is to be

   a restricted
   b unruly
   c subtle
   d ruddy

10. A short battle is called a

   f personification
   g pshaw
   h mutual
   j skirmish

Name ______________________________ Skill: Vocabulary

DIRECTIONS:
Read each sentence and the answer choices. Choose the word or phrase that best completes the sentence. Mark the answer you have chosen.

1. A high tower in a castle is a

   a legacy
   b turret
   c pun
   d outdistance

2. A word that means "to cancel out or get rid of" is

   f fray
   g dunk
   h void
   j fraud

3. To oversee something is to

   a delegate
   b holster
   c emit
   d supervise

4. A person who is regretful or sorry is

   f clogged
   g rueful
   h considerable
   j bribed

5. A word that means "to earn" is

   a recycle
   b merit
   c trodden
   d tidbits

6. To speak out loud is to be

   f jostled
   g vocal
   h persevering
   j loyal

7. A person who helps another learn is a

   a guidance
   b delusion
   c tutor
   d fireman

8. Half of a circle is a

   f fanfare
   g contemporary
   h algebra
   j semicircle

9. An ideal place is a

   a paradise
   b adjoining
   c victorious
   d tedious

10. Something that is useless is

   f unending
   g significant
   h futile
   j robust

Name ______________________________ Skill: Vocabulary

DIRECTIONS:
Read each sentence and the answer choices. Choose the word or phrase that best completes the sentence. Mark the answer.you have chosen

1. Disrespect or open disobedience for a rule is an example of

   a submerge
   b contempt
   c rebellious
   d recollection

2. An amount that is more than enough is

   f percentage
   g haughty
   h inseparable
   j ample

3. To make unfair or selfish use of is to

   a dishevel
   b exploit
   c domesticate
   d contradict

4. A person who breaks in where he is not expected or wanted is an

   f enthusiast
   g acrobat
   h intruder
   j enchantress

5. Anything that came before or happened earlier was

   a fertile
   b prior
   c limitless
   d potential

6. A person who helps another in some act is an

   f umpire
   g officer
   h inconvenience
   j accomplice

7. A deep opening or crack in the earth is a

   a hoax
   b iguana
   c electron
   d chasm

8. A person who keeps totally to themselves is called a

   f ballast
   g ailment
   h hermit
   j congregation

9. To be stubborn is to be

   a identical
   b obstinate
   c gorgeous
   d grotesque

10. A mixture of thought and tender feelings for something is

   f sentiment
   g protrude
   h unmistakable
   j strenuous

Name ______________________________ Skill: Vocabulary

DIRECTIONS:
Read each sentence and the answer choices. Choose the word or phrase that best completes the sentence. Mark the answer you have chosen.

1. When everyone votes the same way it is

   a reverent
   b unyielding
   c sarcasm
   d unanimous

2. To look like something or someone else is to have a

   f persecution
   g resemblance
   h lineage
   j grimace

3. A word that means "deep" is

   a delirious
   b profound
   c descriptive
   d corduroy

4. A sign of things to come is an

   f apprehension
   g awkwardness
   h overload
   j omen

5. Anything that is messy or unkempt is in

   a peril
   b moderate
   c disarray
   d closeness

6. To sleep lightly is to

   f slumber
   g perceive
   h lavish
   j induce

7. To have very strong feelings about something is to have

   a facility
   b fellowship
   c passion
   d discontent

8. Something that is left out is

   f circulation
   g omitted
   h consecutive
   j bearable

9. A person who doubts or is not ready to believe is

   a pompous
   b justified
   c incredulous
   d incorrect

10. A strong feeling or belief is a

   f attachment
   g conviction
   h convulsion
   j conflict

Name ______________________________ Skill: Vocabulary

DIRECTIONS:
Read each sentence and the answer choices. Choose the word or phrase that best completes the sentence. Mark the answer you have chosen.

1. A word that means "sharp or pointed" is

   a acute
   b asylum
   c conjure
   d clarity

2. To be a cautious or a little afraid is to be

   f apprehensive
   g nonchalant
   h precarious
   j profound

3. To set aside for a specific purpose is to

   a rummage
   b dedicate
   c undergo
   d speculate

4. A long time without food is a

   f squire
   g feast
   h famine
   j draught

5. Another word for listen is

   a disable
   b delusion
   c haven
   d hark

6. A ghost or a phantom is an

   f essence
   g expectation
   h apparition
   j indignation

7. To understand is to

   a purify
   b upgrade
   c wallow
   d comprehend

8. A period of ten years is a

   f trickery
   g shortage
   h decade
   j tactic

9. To impede, hold back, or hinder is to

   a recline
   b recede
   c hamper
   d horrify

10. A very useful medicine is

   f detergent
   g penicillin
   h countenance
   j exertion

Name ______________________________ Skill: Vocabulary

DIRECTIONS:
Read each sentence and the answer choices. Choose the word or phrase that best completes the sentence. Mark the answer.you have chosen

1. To make someone angry is to

   a abolish
   b provoke
   c commend
   d compromise

2. To name another person for a position is to

   f nominate
   g guise
   h proposition
   j lacquer

3. A sudden jerk of the muscle is called a

   a tyrant
   b spasm
   c variation
   d scrabble

4. A region or area near or about a place is a

   f zinnia
   g widespread
   h vicinity
   j scallop

5. Something that happens impulsively or without previous planning is

   a scientific
   b intricate
   c spontaneous
   d invalid

6. A book or paper written by hand or with a typewriter is a

   f framework
   g easel
   h manuscript
   j dialogue

7. Something that is clever and useful is

   a progressive
   b ingenious
   c pompous
   d perpetual

8. Things that are happening at the same time are

   f regardless
   g strenuous
   h unhealthy
   j simultaneous

9. When you give a brief statement telling only the main points, you

   a verify
   b summarize
   c reinforce
   d render

10. A person who seems not to care is

    f literal
    g lovable
    h nonchalant
    j preoccupied

Name ______________________________ Skill: Capitalization and Punctuation

DIRECTIONS:
Read each sentence and the answer choices. If there is no error in capitalization or punctuation in the sentence, mark the answer "correct." If there is an error, choose the answer that has the correct capitalization and punctuation.

1. Amy and Susan have a pet hamster. They'll take good care of it.

   a Correct
   b Theyll
   c The'yll
   d Theyw'll

2. The dinosaur's lived on the earth a long time ago.

   f Correct
   g dinosaur'es
   h dinosaurs'
   j dinosaurs

3. The parade crosses pine street then turns on First avenue.

   a Correct
   b Pine Street then turns on First Avenue.
   c pine street then turns on First Avenue.
   d Pine street then turns on First avenue.

4. Please send this package to Mrs Marion M Malone in Brooklyn, New York.

   f Correct
   g Mrs. Marion M Malone
   h Mrs. Marion M. Malone
   j Mrs Marion M. Malone

5. We will take a vacation during the months of june and july.

   a Correct
   b June and July.
   c June. and July
   d June and, July

6. The florida everglades are teeming with wildlife and water plants.

   f Correct
   g Florida, everglades
   h Florida Everglades
   j Florida, Everglades

7. Even after all this time, I want to stay just a little longer.

   a Correct
   b time. I want
   c time; I want
   d time: I want

8. Colin just finished reading the book"mystery at the dead tree"!

   f Correct
   g "Mystery At The Dead Tree"
   h "Mystery at the Dead Tree"
   j "Mystery at the dead Tree"

9. "What are you working on now." asked mother?

   a Correct
   b working on now?" asked mother?
   c working on now?" asked mother,
   d working on now?" asked mother.

10. The plants need attention, will you water them?

   f Correct
   g attention. Will
   h attention, Will
   j attention; Will

Name ______________________________ Skill: Capitalization and Punctuation

DIRECTIONS:
Read each sentence and the answer choices. If there is no error in capitalization or punctuation in the sentence, mark the answer "correct." If there is an error, choose the answer that has the correct capitalization and punctuation.

1. Peter said he <u>couldnt</u> write the story because he had no paper.
   - **a** Correct
   - **b** could'nt
   - **c** couldn't
   - **d** couldno't

2. This <u>books</u> pages are old and torn.
   - **f** Correct
   - **g** bookes
   - **h** book's
   - **j** books'

3. My family took a two week vacation in <u>Toronto, Ontario</u>.
   - **a** Correct
   - **b** Toronto ontario
   - **c** toronto, Ontario
   - **d** toronto, ontario

4. <u>Mr James b frost</u> is the star in this play.
   - **f** Correct
   - **g** Mr. James B frost
   - **h** Mr James B Frost
   - **j** Mr. James B. Frost

5. Let's get together on <u>Monday December 19</u>.
   - **a** Correct
   - **b** Monday december 19
   - **c** monday, December 19
   - **d** Monday, December 19

6. Many types of plants, like the <u>cactus, live in the desert.</u>
   - **f** Correct
   - **g** Cactus, live in the desert.
   - **h** Cactus live in the Desert.
   - **j** cactus live in the desert.

7. Would you care to have <u>Missy and Janice</u> finish painting the wall for you?
   - **a** Correct
   - **b** Missy, and Janice
   - **c** Missy and, Janice
   - **d** Missy and Janice,

8. I like the poem <u>"Seven Gray Squirrels."</u>
   - **f** Correct
   - **g** "seven gray squirrels"
   - **h** "Seven gray squirrels"
   - **j** "seven Gray Squirrels"

9. Herman <u>cried, "Please don't look!"</u>
   - **a** Correct
   - **b** cried! "Please don't look!"
   - **c** cried "Please don't look!"
   - **d** cried, "please don't look!"

10. <u>Sarah cried "I can't</u> hold on another minute more!"
    - **f** Correct
    - **g** Sarah cried! "I can't
    - **h** Sarah cried: "I can't
    - **j** Sarah cried, "I can't

Name ______________________________ Skill: Caplitalization and Punctuation

DIRECTIONS:
Read each sentence and and the answer choices. If there is no error in capitalization or punctuation in the sentence, mark the answer "correct." If there is an error, choose the answer that has the correct capitalization and punctuation.

1. If we are going to the party we'l have to leave soon.
   - **a** Correct
   - **b** w'ell
   - **c** we'll
   - **d** well

2. The dog's collar is too tight.
   - **f** Correct
   - **g** dogs'
   - **h** dog'es
   - **j** dogs'es

3. I have always wanted to visit a foreign city like paris france.
   - **a** Correct
   - **b** paris, france.
   - **c** Paris, France.
   - **d** Paris, france.

4. My new teacher is Mr. Pleason, but he likes to be called JT.
   - **f** Correct
   - **g** j.t.
   - **h** Jt.
   - **j** J.T.

5. Thursdays and fridays are my favorite days of the week.
   - **a** Correct
   - **b** thursdays and fridays
   - **c** Thursdays and Fridays
   - **d** Thursdays, and Fridays

6. Have you ever been to Yellowstone national park?
   - **f** Correct
   - **g** Yellowstone National park
   - **h** Yellowstone national Park
   - **j** Yellowstone National Park

7. It was raining hard. There were puddles all over the lawn.
   - **a** Correct
   - **b** hard, there
   - **c** hard. there
   - **d** hared there

8. My sister's class read the story "Jack and the Beanstalk."
   - **f** Correct
   - **g** play "jack and the beanstalk."
   - **h** play "Jack and the beanstalk".
   - **j** Play "Jack and the beanstalk."

9. "Frank and Roy are the stars of the show!" exclaimed John.
   - **a** Correct
   - **b** of the show" exclaimed John.
   - **c** of the show"! exclaimed John.
   - **d** of the show!" exclaimed, John.

10. The national museum of modern art is a great place to visit.
    - **f** Correct
    - **g** The National museum of modern art
    - **h** The National Museum of Modern Art
    - **j** The national Museum of Modern Art

Name ______________________________ Skill: Grammar

DIRECTIONS:
Read each sentence then read the answer choices. Decide which word or group of words best completes the sentence. Mark the answer you have chosen.

1. We _____ to eat those sandwiches for lunch.
   - **a** was going
   - **b** is going
   - **c** were going
   - **d** going

2. The project that took first place in the contest belongs to _____ .
   - **f** she and I
   - **g** she and me
   - **h** her and me
   - **j** her and I

3. I think that Paula's boots are just a little _____ than mine.
   - **a** smaller
   - **b** smallest
   - **c** more smaller
   - **d** more small

4. How could you _____ that you would not feel well enough to go with us?
   - **f** of knew
   - **g** of known
   - **h** have knew
   - **j** have known

5. This store _____ more jackets than any other store.
   - **a** got
   - **b** gots
   - **c** has
   - **d** have

6. Bobby _____ going to work at the fair this summer.
   - **f** won't
   - **g** weren't
   - **h** aren't
   - **j** isn't

7. The prices of video games _____ each day!
   - **a** were falling
   - **b** was falling
   - **c** falled
   - **d** falling

8. The author of that book will _____ copies at our school today.
   - **f** signing
   - **g** signed
   - **h** been signing
   - **j** be signing

9. We _____ a new song for our school.
   - **a** was writing
   - **b** written
   - **c** has written
   - **d** have written

10. Richard and Quentin _____ sold over one hundred magazines for the school.
    - **f** they both
    - **g** they each
    - **h** each
    - **j** they

Name ______________________________ Skill: Grammar

DIRECTIONS:
Read each sentence and the answer choices. Decide which word or group of words best completes the sentence. Mark the answer you have chosen.

1. The boy _____ when I took his picture.

   a smiled
   b was smiled
   c smile
   d smiling

2. George and his brother _____ the early bus to Detroit.

   f had took
   g have taken
   h has taken
   j has took

3. Phil _____ because he did not wear a warm enough coat.

   a was froze
   b were freezing
   c had frozen
   d was freezing

4. He _____ into the pool before the coach came out of the locker room.

   f doved
   g were diving
   h dove
   j has dived

5. Wendel _____ in many different countries during his lifetime.

   a will living
   b has lived
   c living
   d was lived

6. We will _____ a party for you this Friday.

   f giving
   g gave
   h be giving
   j given

7. We will _____ another mile up the mountain if the weather holds.

   a advancing
   b advanced
   c been advancing
   d advance

8. Hank and Linda _____ going to the dance together.

   f are
   g is
   h be
   j was

9. The medicine _____ the pain quickly.

   a lessen
   b less
   c will lessen
   d will lessening

10. The Smith family _____ camping and won't be back for two weeks.

   f have gone
   g have went
   h has went
   j has gone

Name ______________________________ Skill: Grammar

DIRECTIONS:
Read each sentence and the answer choices. Decide which word or group of words best completes the sentence. Mark the answer you have chosen.

1. We could not _____ it without you!

   a of done
   b of did
   c have done
   d have did

2. Is this assignment _____ a problem for you?

   f gone to be
   g went to be
   h going to be
   j have to be

3. _____ painted all the scenery for the play.

   a Him and me
   b He and I
   c Him and I
   d He and me

4. Kyle _____ this movie four times now!

   f seen
   g has see
   h has seen
   j had saw

5. Susan gave the _____ report in our class.

   a best
   b most best
   c more better
   d bestest

6. Benny _____ many beautiful pictures and is thinking of becoming an artist.

   f has drew
   g has drawn
   h have drawn
   j have drew

7. Vernon _____ riding the bus to work because his car broke down.

   a will
   b am
   c will be
   d were

8. I got _____ books for half price at the book store sale.

   f those there
   g these here
   h those
   j them

9. The children _____ in the park after school.

   a been playing
   b was playing
   c plays
   d were playing

10. The company _____ for a new sales director and my father applied.

   f were advertising
   g had advertise
   h was advertising
   j advertising

Name ______________________________ Skill: Sentence Structure

DIRECTIONS:

Read each group of words and the answer choices. If the group of words makes a complete sentence, mark the space for "Complete sentence". If the group of words is more than one sentence, mark "Run-on sentence". If it is not a complete or run-on sentence, decide which group of words will make the original group a complete sentence. Mark the answer you have chosen.

1. before it gets cold

   a Complete sentence
   b Run-on sentence
   c eat your food
   d and tastes terrible

2. that is a good book

   f Complete sentence
   g Run-on sentence
   h for younger children
   j if you read it

3. driving around the neighborhood

   a Complete sentence
   b Run-on sentence
   c looking for our house
   d he was

4. I read the book it was good

   f Complete sentence
   g Run-on sentence
   h I liked it
   j last week

5. go to bed

   a Complete sentence
   b Run-on sentence
   c before ten o'clock
   d after this movie

6. I held the poster John nailed it to the tree

   f Complete sentence
   g Run-on sentence
   h for the election
   j after we ate

7. between dinner and bed time

   a Complete sentence
   b Run-on sentence
   c do your homework
   d then go to sleep

8. the birds catching worms after the rain

   f Complete sentence
   g Run-on sentence
   h I watched
   j today

9. inside the small brown package

   a Complete sentence
   b Run-on sentence
   c tied with string
   d what is

10. in my red purse with the silver buckles

   f Complete sentence
   g Run-on sentence
   h the money is
   j on the seat of the car

Name ______________________________ Skill: Sentence Structure

DIRECTIONS:
Read each group of words and the answer choices. If the group of words makes a complete sentence, mark the space for "Complete sentence". If the group of words is more than one sentence, mark "Run-on sentence". If it is not a complete or run-on sentence, decide which group of words will make the original group a complete sentence. Mark the answer you have chosen.

1. That green clock on the kitchen wall

   a Complete sentence
   b Run-on sentence
   c is not correct
   d over there

2. wore a beautiful gown to the spring dance

   f Complete sentence
   g Run-on sentence
   h last Friday
   j she

3. it is finally over

   a Complete sentence
   b Run-on sentence
   c and I am glad
   d for this year

4. write the first draft type the final copy

   f Complete sentence
   g Run-on sentence
   h and hand it in
   j if you want

5. the book was very good it took a long time to finish

   a Complete sentence
   b Run-on sentence
   c because it was long
   d I liked it

6. the small boy and his black-and-white spotted dog

   f Complete sentence
   g Run-on sentence
   h went for a walk
   j around the block

7. went around to the back of the house when no one answered the door

   a Complete sentence
   b Run-on sentence
   c the doorbell
   d the visitor

8. Jerry and Glenda

   f Complete sentence
   g Run-on sentence
   h will go
   j tomorrow evening after dinner

9. going to get a part time job at the ice cream parlor

   a Complete sentence
   b Run-on sentence
   c after school
   d she is

10. after dinner we went to a movie

    f Complete sentence
    g Run-on sentence
    h in the mall
    j and liked it

Name ______________________________ Skill: Sentence Structure

DIRECTIONS:
Read each group of words and the answer choices. If the group of words makes a complete sentence, mark the space for "Complete sentence". If the group of words is more than one sentence, mark "Run-on sentence". If it is not a complete or run-on sentence, decide which group of words can be added to make the original group a complete sentence. Mark the answer you have chosen.

1. ice cream with chocolate syrup and whipped cream

   a Complete sentence
   b Run-on sentence
   c we ate
   d and a few chopped nuts

2. watching a show on television

   f Complete sentence
   g Run-on sentence
   h about pollution
   j he was

3. is it warm outside

   a Complete sentence
   b Run-on sentence
   c now that the sun has come up
   d than last night

4. we went shopping I bought a new pair of jeans

   f Complete sentence
   g Run-on sentence
   h and a watch
   j at that store

5. until this class has ended

   a Complete sentence
   b Run-on sentence
   c keep working
   d and the bell has rung

6. Amanda went home

   f Complete sentence
   g Run-on sentence
   h to get her baseball
   j after school

7. in the hallway between classes

   a Complete sentence
   b Run-on sentence
   c they passed
   d and out the door

8. I learned to use the computer it is easy

   f Complete sentence
   g Run-on sentence
   h to learn
   j and lots of fun

9. wanted to win the race so he trained for six weeks

   a Complete sentence
   b Run-on sentence
   c Jason
   d and worked hard

10. the girl with the green and gold skirt

   f Complete sentence
   g Run-on sentence
   h is in my class
   j and gold blouse

Name ____________________ Skill: Reference Skills

DIRECTIONS:
Read each question and the answer choices. Mark the answer you have chosen.

1. Which word would come *first* in alphabetical order?

   a perpetual
   b peril
   c periodical
   d periscope

2. Which word would come *first* in alphabetical order?

   f irresistible
   g involvement
   h iris
   j invest

3. Which word would come *first* in alphabetical order?

   a generator
   b generate
   c gentleness
   d geographical

4. Which pair of guide words would be on the same dictionary page as the word "discern"?

   f disapproval - disclose
   g diminishing - disarray
   h discharge - dislodge
   j decibel - disable

5. Which pair of guide words would be on the same dictionary page as the word "bolster"?

   a bowl - boxcar
   b bandanna - bobcat
   c blunt - bribe
   d bifocal - boisterous

6. Which pair of guide words would be on the same dictionary page as the word "ignite"?

   f identical - idly
   g ignorance - jazz
   h identity - idiom
   j humid - ignorant

7. Where would you look to find if your library has a book about air pollution?

   a card catalog
   b atlas
   c almanac
   d encyclopedia

8. Where in your science book should you look to see if there is a chapter about tectonics?

   f title page
   g glossary
   h Introduction
   j table of contents

9. Where would you look to find how to divide the word "astronomical"?

   a dictionary
   b encyclopedia
   c card catalog
   d atlas

10. Where is the best place to find out which states border Texas?

   f dictionary
   g encyclopedia
   h card catalog
   j atlas

Name ________________________ Skill: Reference Skills

DIRECTIONS:
Read each question and the answer choices. Mark the answer you have chosen.

1. Which word would come *first* in alphabetical order?

   a feud
   b fervent
   c fertile
   d fellowship

2. Which word would come *first* in alphabetical order?

   f hatchet
   g haven
   h hateful
   j haughtily

3. Which word would come *first* in alphabetical order?

   a contradict
   b converse
   c context
   d controller

4. Which pair of guide words would be on the same dictionary page as the word "pore"?

   f pompous - portable
   g periscope - poppy
   h portal - preheat
   j overwork - pollutant

5. Which pair of guide words would be on the same dictionary page as the word "tonic"?

   a tactful - token
   b tedious - tolerate
   c toil - tonsils
   d tunic - turf

6. Which pair of guide words would be on the same dictionary page as the word "vice"?

   f unwanted - vengeance
   g virtual - virtue
   h vapor - visual
   j verge - via

7. Where would you find the most detailed information about China?

   a dictionary
   b encyclopedia
   c table of contents
   d atlas

8. Where would you look to find some titles of books about California?

   f dictionary
   g encyclopedia
   h card catalog
   j atlas

9. Which part of the Spanish book would you use to see on what the word "adios" means?

   a title page
   b glossary
   c Introduction
   d table of contents

10. Where would you look to find the date the book was published?

   f copyright page
   g glossary
   h Introduction
   j table of contents

Name ______________________________ Skill: Reference Skills

DIRECTIONS:
Read each question and the answer choices. Mark the answer you have chosen.

1. Which word would come *first* in alphabetical order?

   a zoologist
   b zoological
   c zipper
   d zinnia

2. Which word would come *first* in alphabetical order?

   f tardy
   g traverse
   h tavern
   j taper

3. Which word would come *first* in alphabetical order?

   a realism
   b razor
   c recollection
   d regal

4. Which pair of guide words would be on the same dictionary page as the word "subdue"?

   f summit - sunless
   g subscribe - suffrage
   h strenuous - stupidity
   j sub - submerge

5. Which pair of guide words would be on the same dictionary page as the word "ballast"?

   a ballet - basically
   b audition - baleful
   c ballad - balm
   d bullet - bumblebee

6. Which pair of guide words would be on the same dictionary page as the word "ecstatic"?

   f dwelt - edible
   g eclipse - economy
   h essence - eventful
   j eliminate - establishment

7. Where would you look to find out how to pronounce a vocabulary word?

   a title page
   b glossary
   c Introduction
   d table of contents

8. Where would you look to find how many meanings the word "exploit" has?

   f dictionary
   g encyclopedia
   h card catalog
   j atlas

9. In which book would you look to find information about boomerangs?

   a dictionary
   b encyclopedia
   c almanac
   d atlas

10. Where would you look to find how many times Patrick Henry is mentioned in a book?

   f title page
   g glossary
   h index
   j table of contents

Name ________________________________ Skill: Reference Skills

DIRECTIONS:
Read each question and the answer choices. Mark the answer you have chosen.

1. Which word would come *first* in alphabetical order?

   a conceive
   b computation
   c conceit
   d compressor

2. Which word would come *first* in alphabetical order?

   f windstorm
   g wind-blown
   h wide-open
   j widespread

3. Which word would come *first* in alphabetical order?

   a strangeness
   b stowaway
   c straightforward
   d stopwatch

4. Which pair of guide words would be on the same dictionary page as the word "ridicule"?

   f reunion - ride
   g rhino - ritual
   h riffle - robust
   j rind - rinse

5. Which pair of guide words would be on the same dictionary page as the word "regal"?

   a regardless - regiment
   b reflector - refusal
   c registration - rejoin
   d recycle - relented

6. Which pair of guide words would be on the same dictionary page as the word "adolescence"?

   f acid - ado
   g acute - adolescent
   h adolescent - adviser
   j activate - adequate

7. In which book would you look to find the states which border Florida?

   a dictionary
   b encyclopedia
   c card catalog
   d atlas

8. Where would you look in your history book to find out what is in chapter three?

   f title page
   g glossary
   h index
   j table of contents

9. Which section of a book lists chapter titles and the pages on which they begin?

   a title page
   b glossary
   c Introduction
   d table of contents

10. Which would you use to locate a particular book on the shelf at the library?

   f dictionary
   g encyclopedia
   h card catalog
   j atlas

Name ______________________________ Skill: Reference Skills

DIRECTIONS:
Use the sample dictionary entries below to answer each question. Mark the answer you have chosen. Mark NH (Not Here) if the question cannot be answered from the information given.

leach [lēch] *(v.)* **1.** run water through slowly; filter: *leach the water through a coffee maker* **2.** dissolve by running water slowly through : *Potash is leached from wood ashes and used to make soap.*

pon•gee [pon jē´] *(n.)* fabric made of soft silk, usually left in a natural brownish-yellow color.

float [flōt] **1.** *(v.)* stay on top of or be held up by water, air or other liquid: *A feather floats on air.* **2.** *(n.)* anything that stays up in water: *A raft is a float.* **3.** *(n.)* a device used to buoy up the end of a fishing line: *Attach the red float to the line.*

sphere [sfir] *(n.)* **1.** any round figure : *That lamp is shaped like a sphere.* **2.** anything representing a star or planet: *That globe is a sphere.* **3.** place or surroundings in which a person exists, works, etc: *The king's sphere of influence extends to the border.*

1. Which entry word would be best to use when talking about filtering?

   a leach
   b pongee
   c sphere
   d NH

2. Which entry word would be best to use when talking about making clothes?

   f float
   g pongee
   h leach
   j sphere

3. Which is the best definition for the word *float* as it is used in this sentence?
   We will build a *float* from these small trees.

   a 1
   b 2
   c 3
   d NH

4. Which is the best definition for the word *sphere* as it is used in this sentence?
   Make a *sphere* from the clay.

   f 1
   g 2
   h 3
   j NH

5. According to this dictionary entry, which part of speech is the word *leach* ?

   a noun
   b verb
   c adjective
   d adverb

6. Which entry words have only one syllable?

   f float, pongee, leach
   g pongee, leach, sphere
   h leach, pongee, float
   j sphere, float, leach

Name ______________________ Skill: Reference Skills

DIRECTIONS:
Use the sample dictionary entries below to answer each question. Mark the answer you have chosen. Mark NH (Not Here) if the question cannot be answered from the information given.

jade [jād] **1.** (*n.*) a hard stone used for jewelry. **2.** (*adj.*) a light green color: *a jade blouse.*

pith•y [pith´ē] (*adj.*) **1.** full of meaning, force or vigor: *a pithy speaker* **2.** constructed of or like pith (spongy tissue found in plants): *the pithy leaves* **3.** having much pith: *a pithy orange*

re•view [ri vyü´] **1.** (*v.*) study again: *Review the lesson.* **2.** (*v.*) look back on: *before falling asleep, she reviewed the meeting.* **3.** (*v.*) look at with care: *A supervisor may review your work before the promotion.* **4.** (*n.*) pre-examination: *The professor will hold a review for the test.*

spoil [spoil] **1.** (*v.*) ruin: *rain will spoil the picnic* **2.** (*v.*) become unfit for use: *the meat will spoil in the sun* **3.** (*v.*) indulge excessively: *spoil the child* **4.** (*n.*) things won or taken by force: *spoils of war*

1. Which is the best definition for the word *pithy* as it is used in this sentence?
   The cucumber was a little *pithy.*

   a 1
   b 2
   c 3
   d NH

2. Which entry word would be best to use when talking about a necklace?

   f review
   g jade
   h pithy
   j spoil

3. Which is the best definition for the word *review* as it is used in this sentence?
   I must *review* for tomorrow's math test.

   a 1
   b 2
   c 4
   d NH

4. Which is the best definition for the word *spoil* as it is used in this sentence?
   The girls' grandfather *spoils* them with gifts.

   f 1
   g 2
   h 3
   j NH

5. According to this dictionary entry, the word *spoil* can be used as which parts of speech?

   a noun and adjective
   b verb and adverb
   c noun and verb
   d NH

6. Which entry word is pronounced exactly as it is spelled?

   f review
   g jade
   h pithy
   j spoil

Name ______________________________ Skill: Reference Skills

DIRECTIONS:
Use the sample dictionary entries below to answer each question. Mark the answer you have chosen. Mark NH (Not Here) if the question cannot be answered from the information given.

ban•quet [bang´kwit] **1.** *(n.)* meal with many courses; feast **2.** (*n*). formal dinner with speeches **3.** (*v.*) take part in a feast: *We banqueted on roast beef and duck.*

scoop [sküp] **1.**(*n.*) tool like a small shovel **2.** (*n.*) part of a power shovel **3.** (*n.*) small amount taken up at one time: *a scoop of sugar* **4.** (*v.*) act of taking up: *scoop up the child* **5.** (*n.*) informal piece of news: *reporter got the scoop.* **6.** (*v.*) hollow or dig out: *scoop melon from the rind*

show [shō] **1.** (*v.*) put in sight: *Show me your hands.* **2.** (*v.*) reveal: *show great fear* **3.** *(v.)* be in sight: *anger showed in his actions.* **4.** *(v.)* point out: *show the way.* **5.** *(v.)* make clear; explain: *show how to do the problem.* **6.** *(n.)* a play or movie: *go to the show.*

wheel•bar•row [hwēl´bar ō] *(n.)* a small vehicle with a wheel at one end and two handles at the other, used for carrying loads.

1. Which is the best definition for the word *show* as it is used in this sentence?
   He *showed* us the best way to get there.

   a 2
   b 4
   c 6
   d NH

2. Which entry word would be best to use when describing a certain small amount?

   f banquet
   g scoop
   h show
   j wheelbarrow

3. Which is the best definition for the word *scoop* as it is used in this sentence?
   Did you hear the *scoop* about the election?

   a 1
   b 5
   c 6
   d NH

4. Which is the best definition for the word *banquet* as it is used in this sentence?
   The *banquet* was very informative.

   f 1
   g 2
   h 3
   j NH

5. According to this dictionary entry, which part of speech is the word *wheelbarrow*?

   a noun
   b verb
   c adjective
   d adverb

6. Which entry word has two long vowel sounds?

   f banquet
   g scoop
   h show
   j wheelbarrow

Name ____________________ Skill: Narrative Passages

DIRECTIONS:
Read each passage. Then, read each question and the answer choices. Mark the answer you have chosen. Mark NH (Not Here) if the question cannot be answered from the information in the passage.

Joan and I started down her front walk. We were on our way to the library to work on a research report. As we passed her neighbor's house we heard a sort of scream. I say a "sort of scream" because it ended abruptly. Joan and I stopped and looked at each other.

"What do you suppose that was?" I asked.

"It came from Mrs. Lang's house," answered Joan. "She is an older lady who lives by herself. Do you think she's alright?"

I gulped and quickly looked away. We needed to do something, but we really couldn't do anything by ourselves. Somebody obviously needed help, and we were the only people who knew about it. I looked up and down the street. There wasn't a soul anywhere. "When will your mom be at home?" I asked.

Joan shook her head. "Both of my parents are at work and won't be home for another hour or two. What should we do?"

We were trying to decide who to call when we heard another noise from Mrs. Lang's house. This time, it was laughter. It was very loud and shrill. Then we heard a voice say, "Get the phone! Get the phone!" The voice was strange and very loud. I was not scared anymore. I started up Mrs. Lang's walk. "Let's ring the bell and see if she is alright. Maybe there is nothing to worry about." I spoke calmly, but inside I was excited. I rang the bell and waited.

Finally the door opened. Mrs. Lang came out onto the porch. "Hello there!" she said.

"We were passing by and heard a strange noise. We just wanted to make sure you were alright." I tried to look past Mrs. Lang into the house.

"Come in, girls!" Mrs. Lang said. "I have a new pet you should meet, and he's a very loud fellow." Just inside the door sat a huge bird cage—with an enormous grey parrot inside.

1. Where were the girls going when they heard the scream?

   a to Joan's house
   b for a walk to the park
   c to the library
   d NH

2. What is the next noise that the girls hear?

   f laughter
   g a voice saying, "Get the phone!"
   h the telephone ringing
   j NH

3. Which of these statements about the story is completely true?

   a Mrs. Lang is hurt
   b the girls were afraid at first
   c The girls think someone is playing a joke
   d NH

4. Why did the voice the girls heard sound strange?

   f it was too loud
   g Mrs. Lang was watching television
   h it was a parrot's voice
   j NH

5. Why don't the girls get Joan's parents to help?

   a they are out shopping
   b they are at work
   c they are on vacation
   d NH

Name ______________________________ Skill: Narrative Passages

DIRECTIONS:
Read each passage. Then, read each question and the answer choices. Mark the answer you have chosen. Mark NH (Not Here) if the question cannot be answered from the information in the passage.

Nathan sat as still as he could on the shaky tree branch. There was no telling what might happen if those bandits looked up and saw him there. Was it just this morning that Nathan had left the cabin so happy about his good luck?

Nathan had arisen with the sun. He didn't want to waste a single minute of this day! He had taken care of the place by himself for the past two weeks. Ma and Pa had been gone for two weeks to visit relatives, and Nathan had been left in charge of the cabin. He mended the fence, tended to the animals, and took care of the all the chores. His parents were proud of the way he had handled everything, so they were giving him this whole day to do whatever he liked. It was a great thing to have so much freedom for an entire day!

But that was before the bandits arrived. Nathan had taken a quick swim. Then he climbed this tree and pretended to be a pirate climbing the rigging of his ship. That is when the bandits rode up on their horses. They stopped under the tree. Nathan could not help listening in on their conversation. He heard them talk about how they had just robbed the bank in a nearby town. He sat very still and watched as they buried the saddle bags full of money under the tree then covered the dirt with a pile of stones. He hardly dared to breathe as he listened to their plans about splitting up and returning to this spot later.

What was Nathan to do? He could not let the bandits see him, but he had been sitting still for so long that his arms and legs were aching. Nathan gently tried to shift his position on the branch. A few leaves broke loose and floated to the ground, landing on one bandit's hat.

1. Why was Nathan in the tree?

   a it was his day off
   b he was building a tree house
   c he was playing pirate
   d NH

2. Why had Ma and Pa left him alone for two weeks?

   f they wanted him to do the chores
   g to visit relatives
   h they went to town for supplies
   j NH

3. Why was Nathan afraid of the bandits?

   a they were thieves
   b they had killed the marshall
   c they were looking for him
   d NH

4. Where did the bandits bury the bags of money?

   f near the river
   g on the farm
   h under the tree
   j NH

5. What happened when Nathan moved a little because he was sore?

   a the bandits looked up at him
   b leaves fell
   c he sneezed
   d NH

Name ______________________________ Skill: Narrative Passages

DIRECTIONS:
Read each passage. Then, read each question and the answer choices. Mark the answer you have chosen. Mark NH (Not Here) if the question cannot be answered from the information in the passage.

Every time I asked my dad if I could have a pet he would answer with a resounding "NO!" I had given him all my best arguments about how a guy my age needed a pet to take care of. I had promised to be responsible and not bother my dad about anything that my pet might need, but he still refused. He said he just did not want a pet around the house.

One day I was sitting on the front steps reading a sports magazine when I smelled something pretty bad. I looked down and saw a scraggly puppy sitting at my feet. The pup looked as if he had spent a week in someone's trash can, and he smelled like it as well. The puppy wagged his tail and put a paw on my shoe. I had to laugh because the expression on his face told me he really needed a friend. "Come on fellow," I smiled. "You need a bath!"

I got the dish detergent and an old brush from the laundry room. I took the puppy to the back yard and turned the hose on him. The puppy looked surprised and not too happy about it, but he did not even try to leave. I soaped him down and scrubbed every bit of garbage and stink from his coat. When he was rinsed and brushed he looked a lot better.

The puppy followed me around for the rest of the afternoon. I didn't say much to him, but it was evident that he wanted to be my dog. Finally, I heard Dad pull into the driveway. He came up the front steps and frowned at me. Without saying a word he looked down at the puppy. The puppy looked up at my dad and slowly wagged his tail. He seemed to know that my dad was not happy about seeing him there. The puppy suddenly laid down and rested his head right across my dad's foot. I was surprised to hear my dad burst out with laughter. "And who do you think you are, dog?" My dad bent and scratched the pup behind the ears. "What are you going to call him?" Dad asked.

1. How did dad feel about getting a pet?

   a he didn't think his son was old enough
   b he didn't want any pets
   c he wanted to wait for a special pet
   d NH

2. How did the boy in the story try to convince his dad he needed a pet?

   f all the other boys had one
   g he promised to be responsible
   h he told his dad he just had to have one
   j NH

3. How do you know that the puppy wanted to belong to the boy?

   a it did not run away
   b it looked hungry
   c it looked surprised and not too happy
   d NH

4. What does dad do that shows he likes the puppy?

   f he frowned
   g he looked down at the puppy
   h he scratched the puppy's ears
   j NH

5. What would be a good title for this story?

   a How I Got My Dog
   b The Black Puppy
   c Dad Says, "No Pets Ever!"
   d NH

Name ______________________________ Skill: Narrative Passages

DIRECTIONS:
Read each passage. Then, read each question and the answer choices. Mark the answer you have chosen. Mark NH (Not Here) if the question cannot be answered from the information in the passage.

It was the weekend at last, and Joel and Erik were out for a day of adventure. The boys were heading for a small island in the middle of Lake Maribu. They could barely see the dot of land from the shore, but they were sure it would be a great place to explore. The boys had heard many stories about that island and the pirates that had visited there years ago. Many people had dug around on the island looking for buried treasure, but none had ever been found. Joel and Erik were certain that the treasure did exist, and they wanted a chance to look for it.

They put their lunch and two shovels into their rowboat and pushed away from the dock. Joel and Erik took turns rowing the boat across the lake. It was a lot further than it looked, and both boys were tired long before they reached the sandy shore of the island.

The island was quite small, about a quarter mile square, and had only a few tall trees. Most of the ground was covered with thick bushes that were covered with small thorns. The boys wondered how a shovel could ever break through those bushes. As Joel and Eric looked over the island, they knew this job was not going to be as easy as they had planned!

After a short rest, Joel picked up a shovel and began to dig on the beach. Erik figured the pirates would have buried the treasure in the middle of the island, so he started off to find a place of his own. The thorns caught at his clothes and made it difficult for Erik to go very far. Just as he was about to give up and turn back, Erik felt his shoe land on something hard and sharp. He stepped back and looked down. There between two thorny bushes the corner of a wooden box showed above the sandy soil. Erik could not believe his eyes! Was this really a treasure chest?

1. What are the boys hoping to find on the island?

   a gold and silver
   b pirate's treasure
   c a skull and crossbones flag
   d NH

2. What did the boys take with them in the boat?

   f water and lunch
   g a radio and lunch
   h two shovels and lunch
   j NH

3. Why was finding the treasure more difficult than they had imagined?

   a it was very hot
   b the thorny bushes made it difficult to dig
   c the island was too large for the search
   d NH

4. What did Erik stumble upon?

   f the pirate's treasure chest
   g a sharp rock
   h a wooden box
   j NH

5. In what time of year does this story take place?

   a spring
   b summer
   c autumn
   d NH

Name ______________________________ Skill: Narrative Passages

DIRECTIONS:
Read each passage. Then, read each question and the answer choices. Mark the answer you have chosen. Mark NH (Not Here) if the question cannot be answered from the information in the passage.

Our class decided to plan a special lunch for our fathers. The teacher agreed to the idea, but said we would have to do all the work. She did not want our parents to do the shopping and the cooking for this lunch!

The first thing we did was plan the menu. It was fun to suggest fancy dishes that we knew our dads would like, but the teacher reminded us who was going to prepare this meal, and the menu suddenly became very plain. We finally decided on spaghetti with meatballs, bread, and a salad. That seemed simple enough for us to put together.

Next we had to make a grocery list of the things we would need. This part was more difficult. Our teacher let us buy the spaghetti, of course, but she wanted us to make our own sauce and mix our own meatballs. We actually had to get the ingredients from a recipe and put things together and do the cooking! We also needed to think about little things you take for granted around the house—like pots, bowls, plates, eating utensils, and napkins.

By the time we were ready to shop, it was evident that our "fun project" was really turning into a learning experience! Buying the groceries also provided a lot of lessons. We had to read the labels and choose the best products we could while staying within our budget. Since our budget was very small, it took a long time to find everything we needed at a good price.

Cooking the food was a blast. We all had a great time mixing the meatballs and adding spices to the sauce. Everyone was careful to follow the directions. We had put a lot effort into this project and did not want to mess it up now!

We were nervous when the dads sat down at our table that day. Would they like the food? Yes, they really did! It was a satisfying meal for every one of us.

1. What project did the class decide to do?

   a plan a menu
   b shop for groceries for a lunch
   c plan a fathers' lunch
   d NH

2. What did they learn about planning a menu?

   f keep it simple
   g don't take things for granted
   h fancy menus are the best
   j NH

3. When the children picked this project they expected to just have fun. What happened?

   a it was too much work and they hated it
   b it turned into a learning experience
   c cooking was too difficult for them
   d NH

4. What made the shopping so difficult?

   f they couldn't find the best products
   g the store was out of pasta
   h they could not spend a lot of money
   j NH

5. What phrase would best describe how the students felt about this project?

   a "No one enjoyed it except the teacher."
   b "It was harder than we thought, but fun!"
   c "It was not worth all the trouble."
   d NH

Name ______________________________ Skill: Narrative Passages

DIRECTIONS:
Read each passage. Then, read each question and the answer choices. Mark the answer you have chosen. Mark NH (Not Here) if the question cannot be answered from the information in the passage.

I remember it all so clearly now. The sky was a beautiful deep blue without a single cloud. The sun was shining brightly, but the cool breeze kept us from becoming too hot. The sand felt warm and soft on my bare toes. The waves made a sound like wind in the trees as it gently slapped at the shore. It was such a great day to be at the beach with my friends.

I sat down on my blanket and prepared to get a tan. I was covered in suntan lotion and had on my favorite sunglasses as I laid back and relaxed. I closed my eyes and listened to all the noises around me. It is surprising what you can hear when you are not using your eyes. I could hear pounding feet as children raced from the water to the blanket where their moms were sitting. I could hear people talking and laughing from quite a distance as the wind carried their voices across the water and the sand. I could hear the water splashing and bubbling with swimmers, and the wind rushing past umbrellas and lawn chairs. And somewhere within all those pleasant sounds I heard something else... something that didn't quite fit.

I am not certain if I heard a shout or not, but I suddenly sat straight up and my eyes few open. Something was wrong. I scanned the beach and the edge of the water, but saw nothing amiss. I put my hand up to shield my eyes from the sun and looked further out in the water. There just beyond the safety buoy I thought I saw a ball or something bobbing in the waves, but it wasn't there now. I kept my eyes on the spot and it suddenly reappeared. I could see someone's head barely above the water, and an arm raised feebly then sank as a wave broke over it.

I raced to the lifeguard station, hoping it would not be too late. The lifeguard looked where I was pointing and took off running toward the water.

1. Where was the narrator of this story?

   a at the pool
   b at a lake
   c at a beach
   d NH

2. How did the narrator become aware that there was a problem?

   f she saw a swimmer too far out
   g she heard something that didn't fit
   h she heard the lifeguard calling
   j NH

3. Where was the person who was in trouble?

   a near the wharf
   b close to the reef
   c not far from a buoy
   d NH

4. What did the narrator do to help the swimmer?

   f threw him a safety buoy
   g swam out to help
   h got a lifeguard
   j NH

5. The narrator listened to "pleasant sounds." Which of the following was <u>not</u> in the story?

   a pounding feet
   b wind carrying voices
   c beach balls being smacked
   d NH

Name ________________________________ Skill: Narrative Passages

DIRECTIONS:
Read each passage. Then, read each question and the answer choices. Mark the answer you have chosen. Mark NH (Not Here) if the question cannot be answered from the information in the passage.

Josey had never ridden a horse before, and she wasn't all that sure that she wanted to ride one now. Her friend, Susie, was eagerly swinging up onto one of those big beasts. She grinned at Josey and stuck out her tongue. Josey knew that was Susie's way of daring her to come along. Even with a dare aimed at her, Josey was not quite ready to give this a try.

The man who owned the horses explained a couple things to Susie then turned to Josey. "Which horse would you like?" Josey looked at the four horses standing near the gate. They looked entirely too large for a person her size.

"Which one is the gentlest?" she asked.

The man laughed and took the reins of a spotted pony. "None of them will give you any trouble, but Buttercup here is as gentle as a lamb." Josey stepped up to the horse and nervously slid her foot into the stirrup. The man boosted her into the saddle.

Josey had not realized how wide a horse was. Her leg muscles hurt, and it sure looked like a long way to the ground. Again she wished she had not let Susie talk her into this silly adventure. The man began to speak, "The horses know the path, so you can't get lost. They'll take you through the woods, down by the lake, and bring you back through that field over there. Just give the horse its head and you can't go wrong." With that he slapped the horse's rump and the trip began.

1. Why isn't Josey excited about riding the horse?
   - **a** she doesn't like this horse
   - **b** she has never ridden before
   - **c** the horse looks pretty wild
   - **d** NH

2. Which word does <u>not</u> describe how Josey is feeling right now?
   - **f** confident
   - **g** anxious
   - **h** nervous
   - **j** NH

3. How did Susie dare Josey to get on the horse?
   - **a** she said "I dare you"
   - **b** she laughed at Josey
   - **c** she stuck out her tongue
   - **d** NH

4. Where does the path take the riders?
   - **f** to the lake and through a field
   - **g** up the mountain and back
   - **h** around the lake and through the pasture
   - **j** NH

5. What is the color of the horse Susie is riding?
   - **a** brown
   - **b** black
   - **c** spotted black and white
   - **d** NH

6. What did the man tell Josey about the horses?
   - **f** they were barrel riders in the rodeo
   - **g** they are very large
   - **h** they know the way around the path
   - **j** NH

Name ______________________________ Skill: Narrative Passages

DIRECTIONS:
Read each passage. Then, read each question and the answer choices. Mark the answer you have chosen. Mark NH (Not Here) if the question cannot be answered from the information in the passage.

Craig picked up the catalog once again. It was so worn that it fell to the right page without Craig even trying. There at the top was the gleaming red bike he had dreamed about for the past three weeks. Craig knew every feature on that bike. It was exactly what he wanted to own, but he didn't have any money. He had begged his parents to buy the bike for him, but they said he didn't need such an expensive toy. But to Craig, it was much more than a toy. This bike was everything he had ever wanted rolled into one.

He lovingly ran his hand over the picture then closed the catalog with a sigh. How was he ever going to be able to afford such an expensive item? He knew he had to find a way to earn the money, but how? He was not old enough to get a job in a store. It would take him more than a year to save enough allowance for it. No, he needed to get some kind of job.

Craig decided to take a walk while he thought about this problem. He walked down the driveway and turned left. Mr. Whitney was out front in his yard trimming the bushes. He waved tiredly and greeted Craig as he wiped the sweat from his forehead.

Across the street Miss Wheatly was taking out the lawn mower. Craig chuckled to himself when she pulled on the cord and the motor barely turned over. He went up to the lawn mower and gave the cord a solid yank. The motor roared to life. "Thanks Craig," shouted Miss Wheatly.

Three houses down Mrs. Gothard was raking up the dead leaves that had gathered by the fence during the winter. Craig couldn't help but notice how hot and tired she looked. Suddenly he got a great idea. The neighbors all needed help, and he needed a job. Could this be the answer he was looking for?

1. What was in the catalog that Craig kept looking at?

   a toys
   b a green bike
   c an expensive red bike
   d NH

2. Why didn't Craig's parents get the bike for him?

   f they couldn't afford it
   g he already had a bike
   h they said he didn't need it
   j NH

3. How could Craig get the bike?

   a get a job at a store
   b save his allowance
   c earn the money
   d NH

4. How did the neighbors help Craig come up with an idea for earning money?

   f they all needed help of some kind
   g they talked to him about his problem
   h they asked him if he wanted a job
   j NH

5. How long will it take Craig to earn the money he needs for the bike?

   a a few weeks
   b two months
   c over a year
   d NH

Name ___________________________ Skill: Narrative Passages

DIRECTIONS:
Read each passage. Then, read each question and the answer choices. Mark the answer you have chosen. Mark NH (Not Here) if the question cannot be answered from the information in the passage.

It was the day after Caroline's thirteenth birthday. She had gotten many nice presents, but her favorite was the ring she now wore on her right hand. Her parents had given her a beautiful opal, which was her birthstone. They said she was responsible enough to own some nice jewelry now, and Caroline was proud that they felt that way.

She had worn the ring to school today. Her friends admired it, and Caroline felt very special with it on her finger. She was very careful with the ring. She knew that opals are soft stones and that they will chip or crack if they bang against harder objects. Caroline put the ring in her purse during gym class to avoid any problems like that! This was such a special ring and Caroline intended to keep it that way.

Each night after dinner Caroline and her sister washed and dried the dishes. Tonight it was her turn to wash. Caroline carefully removed her ring and set it on the window sill above the sink. She filled the sink with soapy water and began to wash the dishes. As they worked, the girls talked about the birthday party and the wonderful presents. Caroline moved her ring a little closer to the edge of the window sill so she could see it sparkle a little better.

The dishes were washed so Caroline pulled the plug in the sink to let the water out. She reached up with her soapy hands and picked up the opal ring. Suddenly the ring slipped from her wet fingers and fell with a plop into the water. Caroline frantically thrust her hands into the water to grab the ring, but she could not find it. She quickly stuck the plug back in the drain to stop the water from rushing out. She parted the bubbles and peered into the water, trying to catch a glimpse of the ring.

1. For what special occasion did Caroline get the ring?

   a her sixteenth birthday
   b her seventh grade graduation
   c her thirteenth birthday
   d NH

2. Which word best describes the way the ring made Caroline feel?

   f fateful
   g dubious
   h grown-up
   j NH

3. Why did Caroline set the ring on the window sill?

   a to hide it from her little sister
   b to protect it while she washed dishes
   c it was beginning to hurt her finger
   d NH

4. Where is the ring at the end of the story?

   f on the window sill
   g in the water under the bubbles
   h down the drain
   j NH

5. What word best describes how Caroline is feeling at the end of this story?

   a unwelcome
   b resourceful
   c panic-stricken
   d NH

Name ______________________________ Skill: Narrative Passages

DIRECTIONS:
Read each passage. Then, read each question and the answer choices. Mark the answer you have chosen. Mark NH (Not Here) if the question cannot be answered from the information in the passage.

Elly, Mike, Roger, and Alyssa were cousins. They were spending a week together at their grandparents' farm. The first few days they explored the barns, fields, and woods around the house. The next two days they helped out with the chores and fed the animals. Now, on the fifth day, they didn't know what to do with themselves.

"Let's take another walk in the woods," suggested Elly. "We can take a picnic lunch and eat by the pond." The children agreed so they packed a lunch and set out.

They talked and laughed as they found a place in the sun near the water's edge. After eating they quieted down, running out of things to say. Alyssa watched a butterfly flit from flower to flower on the far side of the pond. Mike stared into the woods pretending he was a mighty explorer, and the trees were the dense wilderness. Elly pulled pieces of the long grass and wove them together into bracelets. Roger, who was a little bored, began to wander aimlessly around the pond.

Splash! Roger had frightened a turtle that had been sunning itself on the grassy bank. He watched as the turtle dove under the water and disappeared. Suddenly he had a great idea.

"Hey," he called to the others. "Let's catch turtles and have a turtle race!" The group came to life with the idea of such a race. They jumped to their feet and began looking for the tiny reptiles that lived in the pond.

1. What is the relationship among the four characters in this story?

   a they are friends
   b they are neighbors
   c they are cousins
   d NH

2. How long will they stay at their grandparents farm?

   f one week
   g a few days
   h five days
   j NH

3. At the beginning of the fifth day, which word best describes how the children are feeling?

   a glum
   b restless
   c gleeful
   d NH

4. Which words in the story tell you one of the children is a daydreamer?

   f "wove them together into bracelets"
   g "watched a butterfly flit"
   h "pretended he was a mighty explorer"
   j NH

5. Who came up with the idea of having a turtle race?

   a Roger
   b Alyssa
   c Mike
   d NH

6. How many turtles did the children catch?

   f four
   g five
   h six
   j NH

Name ____________________ Skill: Narrative Passages

DIRECTIONS:
Read each passage. Then, read each question and the answer choices. Mark the answer you have chosen. Mark NH (Not Here) if the question cannot be answered from the information in the passage.

The little blue bird sat atop the wooden fence and surveyed the yard carefully. Its sharp eyes could see the movement of a worm in the grass from across the yard. There was very little movement in the grass today, however. The weather had been pretty dry lately, so most of the worms and larger insects had burrowed deeper into the soil. The bird knew this was going to be a slow food day.

As she hopped along the fence eyeing the lawn, the bird spotted a lump of something brown half hidden behind the azalea bush. What could that be? She flew down to get a better look.

She landed a few feet from the bush and poised herself for take-off in case the lump was a cat or other enemy of hers. It was quickly obvious that the brown pile was not an animal. The bird hopped closer and looked again. The "lump" turned out to be a pile of pecan nuts that some squirrel had probably buried last fall. The shells were smooth and uncracked, so the bird reasoned that the meat inside was probably still good.

The little bird had never before eaten a nut. She had watched her cousins, the blue jays, crack open shells like these with their sharp beaks and enjoy the meaty nut inside. She wondered if she might not like nuts too, especially when she was so hungry.

She hopped over and picked up a pecan from the pile. She rolled it across the ground and wondered how to go about cracking it open. Her bill was not so sharp and tough as a blue jay's. She picked up the nut and flew back to the top of the fence. She placed the nut in the crack between two boards and tapped it firmly until it was stuck. Now she could concentrate on getting the shell open.

1. What is this story about?

   a a little bird and a blue jay
   b a bird catching worms
   c a hungry little bird
   d NH

2. At first, what did the bird think the brown lump by the bushes might be?

   f an azalea bush
   g a cat
   h a worm
   j NH

3. Why weren't there many worms for the small bird to eat?

   a bigger birds had gotten them all
   b the worms knew the bird was there
   c they had gone deeper into the ground
   d NH

4. Why would this bird have a hard time cracking the nut shell?

   f her beak was not strong or very sharp
   g she was weak with hunger
   h the nut was impossible for birds to crack
   j NH

5. How did the bird crack the nut shell?

   a pushing it between two boards
   b she hammered it open with her beak
   c she rolled it under a car tire
   d NH

Name ____________________

Skill: Narrative Passages

DIRECTIONS:
Read each passage. Then, read each question and the answer choices. Mark the answer you have chosen. Mark NH (Not Here) if the question cannot be answered from the information in the passage.

Paul awakened suddenly from his sleep. Why did he have to remember his football right now? He looked at the clock and discovered that he had been in bed only an hour. The house was quiet, and he realized that everyone else was in bed and probably asleep by now.

Paul had left his football in the driveway a few weeks ago, and his father had backed over it with the car. His father promised to buy a new one if Paul would promise to take better care of it. The deal was made, and Paul had gotten his new football just two days ago.

Just before dinner Paul and his neighbor, Pete, were tossing the ball back and forth over the fence between their yards. Pete had been called in to dinner, and Paul set the ball down so he could do something else for awhile. Somehow Paul had forgotten to pick the ball up and put it away. Now, at eleven o'clock at night, he remembered.

Paul rolled over and decided to get the ball in the morning, but a loud clap of thunder made him change his mind. He didn't want to leave the new ball out in the rain all night. He sighed with disgust, grabbed his bathrobe, and headed for the back door.

Paul pulled open the door and stepped out into the dark yard. The wind whipped around his legs as he blindly groped his way over to where he had left the ball. He heard a loud noise and realized that the wind had caused the back door to slam shut. Paul grabbed the football and stumbled back to the house. He reached the door just as the clouds opened and buckets of water spilled from the sky.

Paul grabbed the doorknob and pushed, but the door would not open. Paul remembered too late, he had not released the night lock. He was locked out of his own house in the middle of a rainy night!

1. What awakened Paul?

   a the thought of his football outside
   b thunder from the storm
   c the loud wind
   d NH

2. Why did Paul get a new football?

   f his dad gave it to him for his birthday
   g Pete gave it to him
   h the car flattened his old one
   j NH

3. Why did Paul need to get the new ball in the middle of the night?

   a someone might steal it
   b he had promised to take good care of it
   c the car might flatten this one, too
   d NH

4. How did Paul get locked out of the house?

   f his father locked him out as a joke
   g he forgot and closed the door behind him
   h the wind slammed the door closed
   j NH

5. Who is Pete?

   a the main character
   b Paul's father
   c the boy next door
   d NH

Name ______________________________

Skill: Expository Passages

DIRECTIONS:
Read each passage. Then, read each question and the answer choices. Mark the answer you have chosen. Mark NH (Not Here) if the question cannot be answered from the information in the passage.

Sir Isaac Newton was born on January 4, 1643 in England. He lived on a farm with his mother and stepfather but did not work very hard. He preferred to sit and think about things. At that time, people already knew that dropped objects would fall to the ground, but they had no idea why that happened. A popular but untrue story tells of Newton sitting under an apple tree and getting hit on the head by an apple falling from the tree. According to the story, it was at that moment that he discovered gravity. It is highly unlikely that Newton developed the idea of gravity in that way, but Newton is certainly the person who developed the theory of gravitational pull.

Newton explained that gravity is the force that pulls things toward the center of the Earth. Earth has a gravitational pull that attracts even the moon! The sun also has gravity that tries to pull Earth and other planets toward its center.

As people learned about Newton's theory, they accepted the idea of gravity, but wondered why the sun's gravity did not pull Earth right into it. Newton explained this with his theory on centrifugal force. As an object revolves in a circular path (like Earth around the sun), centrifugal force causes the object to pull away from the center of the orbit. A balance between gravity and centrifugal force holds the planets in a steady orbit around the sun.

The theories about gravity and centrifugal force are only two of the theories that Newton developed in his lifetime. He is noted as one of the greatest scientific geniuses of all time because he made important contributions to every major area of science known during his time, including mathematics, physics, optics, and astronomy.

1. How did Newton develop the theory of gravity?
   - **a** an apple fell on his head
   - **b** he worked on his stepfather's farm
   - **c** no one knows for sure
   - **d** NH

2. What is the theory of gravity?
   - **f** a force that pulls things toward the center
   - **g** a force that pulls things away from the center
   - **h** centrifugal force
   - **j** NH

3. What two forces balance the Earth in its orbit around the sun?
   - **a** circular and astronomy
   - **b** mathematics and physics
   - **c** gravity and centrifugal force
   - **d** NH

4. What did Newton like to do instead of work?
   - **f** eat apples
   - **g** sit under trees
   - **h** think about many things
   - **j** NH

5. What area of science is not mentioned in this story?
   - **a** astronomy
   - **b** anatomy
   - **c** optics
   - **d** NH

Name ______________________________ Skill: Expository Passages

DIRECTIONS:
Read each passage. Then, read each question and the answer choices. Mark the answer you have chosen. Mark NH (Not Here) if the question cannot be answered from the information in the passage.

It took nearly 50,000 men two years (1909-1911) to build the famous ship called the *Titanic*. It was a marvel of size and comfort unknown in any other ship at that time. The *Titanic* was 900 ft. (269 m) long, 92 ft. (28m) wide and her eight decks rose to the height of an eleven-story building. The mighty ship weighed 46,328 tons. There were 16 lifeboats aboard, not enough for all the passengers, but more than the law required. The *Titanic* was the largest liner on the seas and was an example of the finest British workmanship. About three million steel rivets held the hull together, and everyone agreed that she was the safest ship afloat. It was so well-built that a shipbuilder's magazine proclaimed that she was "practically unsinkable". From that point on, the *Titanic* became known as "unsinkable".

The *Titanic* was also dubbed the "floating palace" because she was so luxuriously furnished. She boasted four elevators, a gym, heated cabins, barber shops, a library, swimming pool and even an operating room for emergencies! The *Titanic* carried grand staterooms, fancy suites and comfortable cabins for 2,433 passengers. The first class passengers strolled on their own private upper level decks where other passengers were not allowed. The second class passengers were happy on the middle decks with their own private dining rooms and elegant cabins. The bottom levels of the ship were reserved for third class, or steerage. Their cabins held four bunks and a washbasin, which was very elegant for "poor" passengers. No matter which class the passenger was, everyone on board was fed some of the best foods in the world.

On Sunday April 14, 1912, just a few days into her first voyage across the Atlantic ocean, the mighty Titanic struck an iceberg. The "unsinkable" ship became a tragedy at sea.

1. What is the main topic of this story?

   a the sinking of the *Titanic*
   b the building of the *Titanic*
   c a description of the *Titanic*
   d NH

2. How tall was this great ship?

   f 16 stories tall
   g 11 stories tall
   h 92 stories tall
   j NH

3. Why did people feel that the *Titanic* was "unsinkable"?

   a it was so luxurious
   b it was so elegant
   c it was so well-built
   d NH

4. Where were the upper class cabins?

   f on the upper level decks
   g on the middle level decks
   h on the bottom level of the ship
   j NH

5. What does the word "steerage" mean in this story?

   a upper class
   b reserved
   c third class
   d NH

Name ______________________________ Skill: Expository Passages

DIRECTIONS:
Read each passage. Then, read each question and the answer choices. Mark the answer you have chosen. Mark NH (Not Here) if the question cannot be answered from the information in the passage.

Elections are very much a part of our lives. Students elect class officers. Athletic teams elect captains. Clubs, scout troops, and church groups elect chairmen and leaders.

Elections are held to choose a person for a particular job. How does this work? Let's take the example of choosing a 7th grade class president. Candidates, or students who are interested in the position, must let the class members know they are running for that office. They will talk to their classmates and make posters to advertise themselves. The class then has a chance to vote for the candidate of their choice. A ballot will be made to count the votes. A ballot is a piece of paper listing the candidates for president (and any other positions the class may be voting for that day). The students mark their choices on the ballots and turn them in so the votes can be counted. The person who gets the most votes becomes the new class president.

Your parents may belong to some club or organization that nominates candidates and elects officers. The Parent-Teacher Associations at schools do this. Many clubs, organizations, and businesses follow this same procedure.

Companies often determine important rules by elections that are open to all the people who own their stock. Thousands of ballots are mailed to stockholders who vote for their choices and mail them back to the company to be counted. Sports writers follow the weekly records of outstanding football players and, at the end of the season, they vote to select the best in each area to play on an All-Star or All-Pro team. Each spring the members of the Academy of Motion Picture Arts and Sciences cast their ballots to decide who will win the gold statuettes known as Oscars.

Every day elections of one kind or another are taking place. Elections are very much a part of our lives.

1. What is an election?

   a the process of voting for candidates
   b running for office
   c nominating a person for an office
   d NH

2. What does the word "ballot" mean?

   f people interested in an office
   g a list of candidates from which to choose
   h associations or organizations
   j NH

3. Who wins in an election?

   a the person who was the best candidate
   b nominations
   c the person with the most votes
   d NH

4. How old do you have to be to vote in an election?

   f eight
   g eighteen
   h twenty-one
   j NH

5. What does "cast a ballot" mean?

   a throw away a vote
   b vote on a ballot
   c become a candidate
   d NH

Name ________________________________ Skill: Expository Passages

DIRECTIONS:
Read each passage. Then, read each question and the answer choices. Mark the answer you have chosen. Mark NH (Not Here) if the question cannot be answered from the information in the passage.

An astronomer is a person who studies the stars and planets. Today's astronomers have huge telescopes that can show us planets in other galaxies. The first astronomers did not have such instruments. All they had was their eyes and the night sky above them. One of the earliest known astronomers was Pythagoras. He was born in Greece about 560 B.C.

At this time in our history, people were fairly civilized and now had the time to think about the world and how it worked instead of worrying about finding food each day. Pythagoras and a group of other Greeks moved to Croton in southern Italy and set up a school. This group thought about philosophy, religion, mathematics, and science. Pythagoras especially loved mathematics and science. He used these subjects to help develop a theory about the sun and the stars.

Each day Pythagoras would watch the sun rise in the east and cross the sky to set in the west. Because of this, he reasoned that the sun actually circles Earth! He took what he knew about science and decided that Earth must have a massive fire contained deep within its core. This fire is what attracts the sun and makes it revolve, or circle around the earth. He also thought that the other planets and stars revolved around this fire as well.

Although this theory may sound very strange to us now, since we know Earth revolves around the sun, it was the first known time that anyone had tried to explain the relationship between the movement of the sun and Earth. Pythagoras had a lot of correct ideas in his theory: revolution, a ball of fire, planets circling something. Other astronomers took these ideas and added their own information. It took over one thousand years and a lot of astronomers' ideas to arrive at the theory we believe to be true today.

1. Who or what is this story mainly about?

   a Sun and Earth theory
   b astronomers
   c Pythagoras
   d NH

2. According to this story, which subject was not taught at the Croton school?

   f philosophy
   g grammar
   h religion
   j NH

3. What did Pythagoras think was causing the sun and stars to revolve around the Earth?

   a gravity
   b astronomy
   c a ball of fire at the center
   d NH

4. What rotational theory do we believe today?

   f earth-centered (geocentric)
   g self-centered (egocentric)
   h sun-centered (hexocentric)
   j NH

5. What does the word "revolution" mean as it is used in this story?

   a to revolt
   b to spin backwards
   c to circle around
   d NH

Name ____________________ Skill: Expository Passages

DIRECTIONS:
Read each passage. Then, read each question and the answer choices. Mark the answer you have chosen. Mark NH (Not Here) if the question cannot be answered from the information in the passage.

In early times, people did not have calendars to help them keep track of time. They used natural calendars, like bushes, trees, or even insects. Early farmers watched the trees to know when it was time to plant crops. When certain trees began to bud it was a sign that spring was on its way. During the late summer, those farmers would watch for certain insects to appear, indicating that it was time to harvest the crops. Natural calendars were useful to people, but not always accurate. People noticed that the moon made a better calendar.

Astronomers noticed predictable changes in the moon, things that happened in cycles or phases. The moon would seem to grow until it was full and round, and then it would wane until it could not be seen at all. It took about twenty-nine days for the moon to go from full to "new" and back to full. Ancient people called this period of time "month", coming from the Latin word for moon. This cycle repeated itself thirteen times each year, and so the lunar (moon) calendar was invented.

The Romans gave names to all the months. The original names were: *Januarius*, *Februarius*, *Martius*, *Aprilis*, *Maius*, *Junius*, *Quintilis* (later renamed Julius in honor of Julius Caesar), *Sextilis*, *Septembris*, *Octobris*, *Novembris*, *Decembris*, and *Mercedinus*. Eventually, the Romans decided to make the calendar correspond more closely to the solar year. Instead of thirteen months, they observed only twelve. The days of Mercedinus were dispersed among the other months, giving some months thirty days and others thirty-one, making each year 365 days long.

Still, the calendar was off by about one day every four years. The Romans decided to make the year 365 days for three years and 366 on the fourth year. This is the calendar we use today.

1. What are "natural calendars"?

   a using the sun to tell time
   b telling seasons by plants and animals
   c watching the rain or snow
   d NH

2. Using the clues in the story, what does the word "wane" mean?

   f to grow or get bigger
   g to pale or turn white
   h to lose size or get smaller
   j NH

3. About how long does it take the moon to complete one full cycle?

   a 29 days
   b 365 days
   c 31 days
   d NH

4. What group of people supplied the original names for the months of the year?

   f Greeks
   g Romans
   h Germans
   j NH

5. What was the name given to the thirteenth month?

   a Januarius
   b Septembris
   c Decembris
   d NH

Name ________________________________ Skill: Expository Passages

DIRECTIONS:
Read each passage. Then, read each question and the answer choices. Mark the answer you have chosen. Mark NH (Not Here) if the question cannot be answered from the information in the passage.

One of the oldest kinds of plants on Earth is algae. Algae are water plants that can make their own food, but lack stems, leaves, and roots. Some algae are small, one celled plants that form a kind of scum on rocks. Other algae, such as seaweed or kelp, can grow to be quite large. Many kinds of algae are useful to human beings and other animals.

Where ever you find algae, you will find many animals that rely on this plant as their food source. Most small fish live entirely on algae. It also a good source of oxygen which is necessary for life in the water. It is not only small animals that dine on this plant. Even some large animals eat algae—in very large quantities!

In certain parts of the world algae has been used as a base for soups, gelatins, salads, and other foods. Everyone who enjoys ice cream or chocolate milk can thank algae for these treats. A sodium (salt) compound taken from algae is used to keep ice cream smooth and the chocolate from settling at the bottom of the milk.

Algae is also useful in other areas of our lives. Farmers have known for a long time that seaweeds mixed with the soil will replenish the needed salt and iodine that crops absorb. Hospitals use a form of algae as a base for growing and studying bacteria. Algae are used in many things ranging from cosmetics to leather-finishing. Without algae, our lives would definitely be different.

Recently sciences discovered fossil evidence that algae lived millions of years ago, around the same time as the dinosaurs. It is believed that herbivore (plant eating) dinosaurs may have dined on algae, too!

1. What is the main idea of this story?

   a algae is a plant
   b there are many uses for algae
   c dinosaurs ate algae
   d NH

2. How is algae helpful to small fish?

   f it helps keep the water clean
   g as a source of food and oxygen
   h it provides a good hiding place
   j NH

3. Which type of algae was <u>not</u> mentioned in this story?

   a seaweed
   b green algae
   c kelp
   d NH

4. What does algae replace in the soil?

   f iodine
   g cosmetics
   h bacteria
   j NH

5. How do scientists know dinosaurs could have eaten algae?

   a they found algae in dinosaur remains
   b they found algae fossils from that time
   c herbivores had to eat algae
   d NH

Name ____________________ Skill: Expository Passages

DIRECTIONS:
Read each passage. Then, read each question and the answer choices. Mark the answer you have chosen. Mark NH (Not Here) if the question cannot be answered from the information in the passage.

In the early 1800's girls went to school to get a basic education. They learned to read, write, and do math much as they do today. However, young girls were encouraged to learn only the things that would help them become better wives and mothers. They were discouraged from schooling beyond third or fourth grade and were refused a higher education.

Lucy Stone wanted more of an education. As a young child in Massachusetts she gathered nuts and berries to sell and bought schoolbooks that her father refused to get for her. When she became a teen her father ordered her to leave school. Lucy wanted to learn more, and decided that she would go to college. It took Lucy a long time to convince her father to lend her money for a higher education, but he finally did.

Lucy went to Oberlin College in Ohio. Oberlin was the only college in the country open to women and blacks during the 1830's. Although Lucy was a good student, she had to fight for the right to take part in many of the activities open only to men. She wanted to join the debate team and give public speeches, but she was never allowed to do it. Lucy continued with determination and became the first woman from Massachusetts to earn a college degree. After college, she became an advocate for women's suffrage—the right to vote.

1. What would be a good title for this story?

   a Women and Schools
   b Lucy Stone Fights for an Education
   c Only Men Can Go To College
   d NH

2. How did Lucy earn money for school books?

   f she mended clothing
   g she sold berries and nuts
   h she worked for her father
   j NH

3. What did people think girls in the 1800's needed to learn?

   a higher mathematics
   b how to be a good wife and mother
   c how to help run a business
   d NH

4. What college did Lucy Stone attend?

   f Ohio State University
   g University of Massachusetts
   h Oberlin College
   j NH

5. What was unusual about this college in the 1830's?

   a it allowed blacks and women to attend
   b it allowed women to debate
   c it allowed women to give public speeches
   d NH

6. How old was Lucy when her father gave her the money for college?

   f in her early teens
   g seventeen
   h twenty-two
   j NH

Name ______________________________ Skill: Expository Passages

DIRECTIONS:
Read each passage. Then, read each question and the answer choices. Mark the answer you have chosen. Mark NH (Not Here) if the question cannot be answered from the information in the passage.

The first boat was probably a log that a prehistoric man found floating in the water. He climbed up on the log and realized that it would carry him down stream without a lot of effort. But the log was difficult to stay on as it rolled and twisted in the water. When the log was shaped a bit on the bottom and hollowed out for a place to sit, the first true boat was born.

The boat became important as a means of travel. It was discovered that the boat could be guided using oars or paddles that would push against the water. It was the only way to get across an expanse of deep water, and it could carry heavy loads for great distances. For the first time man did not have to depend on animals or his own two feet to get him someplace!

About five thousand years ago, the Egyptians began building large boats made from reeds. These were the first ships. Later they found that wood made stronger ships that would last a lot longer and could carry even more weight. These ships were used to travel the Nile River and seldom went out to sea.

The Greeks and Romans were the first to take sea voyages. Trading ships would sail the Mediterranean taking goods to other countries. These ships had rounded sides and small sails that made them easier to handle in the rough waters.

1. What is this story about?

   a Roman trading at sea
   b how the first boat was invented
   c the early history of boats
   d NH

2. What was probably the first "true boat"?

   f a floating log
   g a hollowed out log
   h a framework covered with animal skins
   j NH

3. Why was the boat so important?

   a it made travel along water easier
   b it saved the animals from a long walk
   c boats were easier to handle than animals
   d NH

4. About what time was the first boat invented?

   f 5000 B.C.
   g 500 B.C.
   h 1000 A.D.
   j NH

5. Which group made the first real ship?

   a Greeks
   b Romans
   c Egyptians
   d NH

6. Which groups were the first to make sea voyages to trade with other countries?

   f Greeks and Romans
   g Greeks and Egyptians
   h Egyptians and Romans
   j NH

Name ____________________________________ Skill: Expository Passages

DIRECTIONS:
Read each passage. Then, read each question and the answer choices. Mark the answer you have chosen. Mark NH (Not Here) if the question cannot be answered from the information in the passage.

The tree frog is an unusual amphibian. Where most frogs live in very wet places, the tree frog prefers the safety of a tree! These frogs are a bright green in color, which allows them to camouflage themselves almost perfectly among the leaves. Most grow to be only one inch long, making them even more difficult for predators to find.

The tree frog has very long toes that have sticky discs on the ends. These discs help the frog cling to slippery bark, leaves, and grass without sliding off. They are even able to cling to glass and have been seen on the outside of many windows at night.

In the early spring these frogs make an appearance. Although they are hard to see because of their green color, they can be heard loud and clear during the night. It is amazing that such a small animal can make such a loud noise! It is their loud calling that earned them the nickname "spring peepers." The reason for their loud voice is the size of their vocal sacs, found between their bottom jaw and their chest. The tree frogs can expand this sac to almost twice the size of their head. With this enormous "drum" they can produce a remarkable sound that carries for long distances.

The eggs are laid in early spring in fresh water and the tiny reddish tadpoles feed on mosquito larvae. Their lungs develop quickly, allowing them to leave the water and live on land sooner than most other frogs. Often they are living on land even before their tadpole tails have completely gone!

1. Where do most frogs prefer to live?

   a under rocks
   b places that are wet
   c in the grass
   d NH

2. What helps a tree frog stay in the tree?

   f the tail does not completely go away
   g a color that is very green
   h the sticky pads on its toes
   j NH

3. Why are these frogs sometimes called "spring peepers"?

   a they make a loud noise in early spring
   b they have large vocal sacs
   c they come in early spring
   d NH

4. What is unusual about tree frog tadpoles?

   f they have no tails
   g they are born with lungs
   h their lungs develop quickly
   j NH

5. What is the average size for an adult tree frog?

   a 2 to 3 inches
   b one centimeter
   c one inch
   d NH

Name ______________________________ Skill: Expository Passages

DIRECTIONS:
Read each passage. Then, read each question and the answer choices. Mark the answer you have chosen. Mark NH (Not Here) if the question cannot be answered from the information in the passage.

A cloud of hydrogen and helium is floating somewhere in space. As it moves it collects bits of dust and more gases that are also floating out there. This "cloud" is called a nebula. As more dust and gases are pulled in, the cloud begins to warm. As the cloud becomes more dense (thick), the heat and friction cause the atoms to explode. The entire cloud ignites and a star is born!

The burning hydrogen fuses to form more helium, and the star slowly expands. The star will burn in this manner for about ten billion years as it radiates heat and energy. When the hydrogen begins to burn out the star becomes even larger, but it is starting to cool. The helium is firmly packed into a core at the middle of the ball of flames. At this stage it gives off a lot of light, but not much energy.

What happens to the star depends on its size. Smaller stars will become white dwarfs, burning brightly until they run out of hydrogen. Large stars often explode as a supernova (burning brightly and quickly). In many cases, the star then burns brightly until it suddenly dies. If the helium core survives the explosion, the dying star might become one of the great mysteries of space—a black hole.

A black hole occurs when the dying star has a large core of helium. The gravity of this dense mass becomes so great it pulls the star into itself! Although a black hole is not really a hole at all, it is so dense and the gravity so great that it is able to pull even light into it. Scientists are not sure they can see a black hole and so cannot prove that they exist, except by looking at the way they affect stars and planets around them. However, the Hubble Space Telescope sent back pictures of a black disk in the center of galaxy M87. It is possible that this disk is a black hole.

1. About how many years does a star burn?

   a 10 thousand
   b 10 million
   c 10 billion
   d NH

2. What gases can be found in a star?

   f oxygen and nitrogen
   g helium and oxygen
   h hydrogen and helium
   j NH

3. Which gas makes up the core of a dying star?

   a nitrogen
   b helium
   c hydrogen
   d NH

4. What is a black hole?

   f a star that has collapsed in on itself
   g a large black hole in space
   h a mass of hydrogen about to explode
   j NH

5. Which of these statements is true according to this story?

   a supernovas are new stars just beginning
   b scientists have a picture of a black star
   c a nebula is a cloud of dust and gases
   d NH

Name ______________________________ Skill: Expository Passages

DIRECTIONS:
Read each passage. Then, read each question and the answer choices. Mark the answer you have chosen. Mark NH (Not Here) if the question cannot be answered from the information in the passage.

Thomas Alva Edison was born in 1847. As a boy, he liked to think about how things worked. He often daydreamed in class and was constantly getting himself into trouble with his teachers. By the time he was in sixth grade, Thomas was failing many subjects. The teachers told his mother that Thomas was a little "addled," or not very bright.

By the time he was twenty-four, Thomas had two inventions that were fairly popular. They earned him enough money to buy a small manufacturing plant in Newark, New Jersey. In 1876 he moved his laboratory to Menlo Park, New Jersey. This is where Edison made some of his most important inventions. It was here that the lightbulb came into being.

Edison had always felt that electricity could be used to produce light. All he needed was some kind of bulb that could harness the energy. But making a lightbulb was harder than he imagined. Edison was ruining glass bulbs faster than the glass blower could make new ones. He used different sizes and shapes, arranged the wires this way and that, but the light never lasted long enough to be useful.

The biggest problem Edison had was the filament, the thin wire that gives off light inside the bulb. It had to be made of something that would glow, but not burn as electricity passed through it. It took over a year to solve the problem and perfect the invention, but in 1879 Edison gave the world the first electric lightbulb.

Among Edison's other inventions were the first motion picture camera, the fluoroscope (the first machine able to "see" inside the body), the mimeograph machine (able to make copies), and an improved battery.

1. Which way might Edison's sixth grade teachers have described him?

   a as a stowaway
   b irresistibly cute
   c dim witted
   d NH

2. How did Edison get the money to buy a business in New Jersey?

   f he worked for an inventor
   g he invented the lightbulb
   h he had two popular inventions
   j NH

3. Which part of the inventing the lightbulb gave Thomas the most difficulty?

   a finding the right shape for the bulb
   b the material for the filament
   c getting the electricity in the bulb
   d NH

4. In what city was Thomas Edison born?

   f Menlo Park
   g Newark
   h Baltimore
   j NH

5. In what year was the lightbulb finally invented?

   a 1847
   b 1871
   c 1879
   d NH

Name ______________________________ Skill: Expository Passages

DIRECTIONS:
Read each passage. Then, read each question and the answer choices. Mark the answer you have chosen. Mark NH (Not Here) if the question cannot be answered from the information in the passage.

Some people seem to be born with great memories. They never forget their assignments, their locker combinations, or anybody's name. How lucky to be born that way! If you don't have a perfect memory, there are a few things you can do to improve it.

First, you need to consciously decide what is important to remember. Think about what is being said and what you need to remember. Not everything your teacher says needs to go into your notebook. Pick out the important facts that will most likely be on the test.

Once you have chosen what you want to remember, you need to store it in your brain. There is not one certain part of your brain where all memories are kept. Memories are filed in many different areas, depending on what they are and how you choose to remember them. Think of the brain as a big file cabinet with many drawers for information. Organizing the information into categories or groups and filing it into the right drawers will help you to remember it later.

Let's look at an example. You have just learned about a breed of dog that is unknown to you: the Irish Wolfhound, and you want to file the information. In your mind you would open the drawer that holds what you know about animals. Inside that drawer you should find files about kinds of animals. One will be types of dogs you know. Put the Irish Wolfhound in that file.

The more places you file something, the easier it will be to remember it when you need it. For example, the Irish Wolfhound has beautiful brown eyes and so does your Aunt Martha. Pairing the new dog with your Aunt Martha when you file it in your brain might not make her very happy, but it will make it much easier to remember that dog when you need to!

1. What is the main topic of this story?

   a the Irish Wolfhound
   b improving your memory
   c people with great memories
   d NH

2. What is the first thing to do before trying to memorize something?

   f pick the important facts to concentrate on
   g write down the important facts
   h try to remember everything at once
   j NH

3. To what does this story compare the brain?

   a a drawer
   b a dog house
   c a file cabinet
   d NH

4. What should you do with new information as you put it into your brain?

   f group it by colors
   g keep it organized and categorized
   h stick it in anywhere
   j NH

5. What color fur does an Irish Wolfhound have?

   a golden
   b black
   c spotted
   d NH

Name ______________________________ Skill: Directions

DIRECTIONS:
Read each passage. Then, read the questions and answer choices. Mark the answer you have chosen. Mark the choice NH (not here) if the question cannot be answered from the information given.

Make S'mores

It is impractical to take all the comforts of a home kitchen with you on a camping trip, but that doesn't mean you cannot have a delicious and simple treat for dessert with a campfire and a few ingredients.

1. Make sure you have a bag of large marshmallows, several plain, milk chocolate bars, and a box of graham crackers.
2. To make a skewer for each camper, peel the bark from one end of a thin tree branch about a yard long. Use a pocket knife, or sandpaper to sharpen the peeled end of the stick.
3. Break each graham cracker in half (the two halves will form the top and bottom of a sandwich). Place a square of milk chocolate on 1/2 of the graham cracker squares.
4. Place a marshmallow on each skewer, and let each camper roast his marshmallow over the campfire until it is melted, but not too burned.
5. Place the hot marshmallow, still on the skewer, gently on top of the graham cracker and chocolate square. Put the other graham cracker on top of the marshmallow and gently squeeze the crackers together, using them to pull the marshmallow off the skewer. Allow the heat from the marshmallow to melt the chocolate, then enjoy!

1. What is the main idea for these directions?

   a cutting branches
   b making a camp dessert
   c making a meal
   d NH

2. Which of the following do you do first?

   f roast marshmallows
   g break graham crackers
   h make a skewer
   j NH

3. What should you do with the branches?

   a break them
   b place them on the top of the fire
   c sharpen the ends
   d NH

4. Why should you use the two halves of the graham cracker to remove the marshmallow?

   f the marshmallow is hot
   g the marshmallow is sticky
   h the marshmallow is slippery
   j NH

5. Which statement below is <u>not</u> discussed in the directions?

   a how many each person should eat
   b how much chocolate to use per cracker
   c what type of chocolate to use
   d NH

6. How long should you roast the marshmallows?

   f until they are melted
   g only a few seconds
   h until they are black and crunchy
   j NH

Name ______________________________ Skill: Directions

DIRECTIONS:
Read each passage. Then, read the questions and answer choices. Mark the answer you have chosen. Mark the choice NH (not here) if the question cannot be answered from the information given.

Finding North

Here is a simple trick that will help you find the direction NORTH.

1. Find a straight stick about 3 or 4 feet long.
2. Set the stick in the ground in a open area where the sun will shine on it.
3. Find the tip of the stick's shadow and mark it on the ground (a small rock works well).
4. Wait a few minutes so the shadow will have time to move. Place another stone at the tip of the shadow.
5. Draw a straight line through both stones.

This line runs east and west. The first stone is at the west end of the line. Stand on the line with the first stone on your left. You are now facing north!

1. What are these directions helping you to do?

   a tell the time of day
   b find the direction north
   c measure the sun's movement
   d NH

2. If you follow the directions, how long will it take to find north?

   f 1 or 2 minutes
   g 10 or 20 minutes
   h 1 or 2 hours
   j NH

3. What materials do you need to follow these directions?

   a grass, a pole, the sun
   b a stick, a ruler, the sun
   c a stick, stones, the sun
   d NH

4. In which step do you draw a line through the rocks?

   f 1
   g 4
   h 5
   j NH

5. To find north, you should stand on the line with which stone to your right side?

   a the biggest stone
   b the first stone
   c the second stone
   d NH

6. Of the following, when wouldn't you be able to use this helpful trick?

   f at noon
   g at 8 o'clock a.m.
   h at night
   j NH

Name ______________________ Skill: Directions

DIRECTIONS:
Read each passage. Then, read the questions and answer choices. Mark the answer you have chosen. Mark the choice NH (not here) if the question cannot be answered from the information given.

Group Picnic Plans

1. The north picnic area is where the seventh grade classes will meet and eat lunch.
2. The south picnic area is where the eighth grade classes will meet and eat lunch.
3. Buses may park in either lot (marked P).
4. Mrs. Gray asks her 8th graders to come to south shelter 4 at 1:30 for a special meeting.
5. There will be a whole group softball game on the field at 11:00.
6. No swimming will be allowed at any time today.
7. The playground will be available for our classes between 9 and 10 a.m.
8. There are two restrooms available (marked R).
9. Buses will leave the park promptly at 2:30.

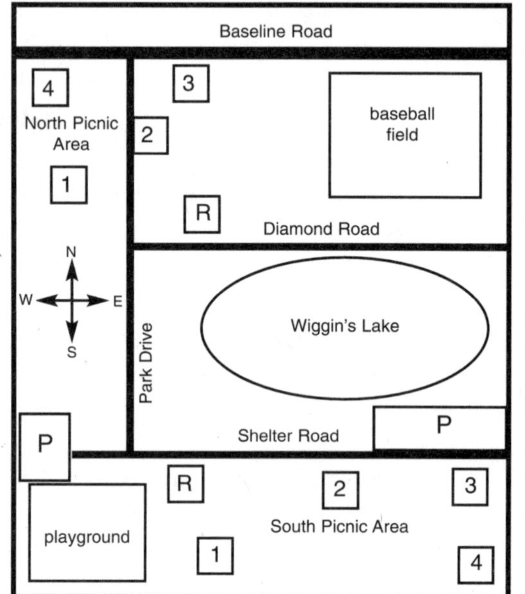

1. Where will the buses park?

   a near the playground
   b near the lake
   c either parking lot
   d NH

2. At what time is the lake opened for swimming?

   f 11:00
   g 1:30
   h 2:30
   j NH

3. Who will play in the softball game?

   a teachers against students
   b seventh grade against eighth grade
   c our school against another school
   d NH

4. What happens at 1:30?

   f a softball game
   g a class meets in south shelter 4
   h the playground is open to our classes
   j NH

5. Where is the eighth grade going to eat lunch?

   a north picnic area
   b south picnic area
   c by the lake
   d NH

6. How many restrooms are in Wiggin's Park?

   f 1
   g 2
   h 3
   j NH

Name ______________________________ Skill: Directions

DIRECTIONS:
Read each passage. Then, read the questions and answer choices. Mark the answer you have chosen. Mark the choice NH (not here) if the question cannot be answered from the information given.

Making a Terrarium

Materials needed: a large container that can be covered (fish bowl, fish tank, gallon jar, etc.), gravel, sand, charcoal, soil, small rooted plants, water.

1. Place a layer of gravel in the bottom of the container.
2. Pour in a layer of sand, making sure the gravel is well covered.
3. A half inch of charcoal is then layered over the sand. These three layers ensure proper drainage for your terrarium.
4. Add 2 or 3 inches of rich soil over the drainage.
5. Add the plants you have chosen for your terrarium. For better growing results, select plants that have a good root system. (Suggested plants that smell great are ferns, partridgeberry, wintergreen, and wild mint. A few crushed pine needles also add a nice fragrance.)
6. Moisten the soil well.
7. Place a cover on the container and keep it in a shady place.

1. How much soil is needed for the terrarium?

   a a thin layer
   b a half inch layer
   c a 2- to 3-inch layer
   d NH

2. Which of the following would not make a good terrarium?

   f glass fish bowl
   g plastic gallon jug
   h a cardboard box
   j NH

3. What can you use to add a little more fragrance to the terrarium?

   a moss
   b charcoal
   c pine needles
   d NH

4. What do the gravel, sand, and charcoal do for the terrarium?

   f feed the plants
   g keep it dry
   h provide drainage
   j NH

5. What should you do in step six?

   a plant the plants
   b add the soil
   c water the plants and soil
   d NH

6. How big are the largest plants you should use?

   f no more than 5 inches tall
   g about a foot tall
   h three feet or taller
   j NH

Name ______________________ Skill: Directions

DIRECTIONS:
Read each passage. Then, read the questions and answer choices. Mark the answer you have chosen. Mark the choice NH (not here) if the question cannot be answered from the information given.

Maple Raisin Pudding

Ingredients:

2 tablespoons softened butter or margarine
1/4 cup sugar
2 eggs
1 1/2 cups all-purpose flour
1 tablespoon baking powder
1/2 teaspoon salt
1/2 cup raisins
1 cup milk
1 1/2 cups pure maple syrup
Whipping cream or ice cream (optional)

Directions

1. In a mixing bowl, cream butter and sugar.
2. Add the eggs, one at a time, beating well after each addition.
3. Combine flour, baking powder, salt and raisins; add alternately with milk to creamed mixture.
4. In a small saucepan, bring syrup to a boil; pour into a greased 1 1/2 quart baking dish.
5. Pour batter over hot syrup; do not stir.
6. Bake, uncovered, at 375° for 30 to 35 minutes.
7. Serve hot with cream or ice cream if desired. Serves 6 to 8.

1. How much flour does this recipe call for?

   a 1 tablespoon
   b 1/2 cup
   c 1-1/2 cups
   d NH

2. How long should you bake the pudding?

   f 30 - 35 minutes
   g 50 - 55 minutes
   h 20 - 25 minutes
   j NH

3. What ingredient is added in step two?

   a sugar
   b milk
   c eggs
   d NH

4. How many people will this recipe feed?

   f one to two and a half
   g six to eight
   h three hundred seventy-five
   j NH

5. What does the baking powder do for this recipe?

   a makes the pudding creamy
   b makes it brown in the oven
   c sweetens the butter
   d NH

6. Which container is used when the pudding is being baked?

   f mixing bowl
   g small saucepan
   h 1-1/2 quart dish
   j NH

Name ______________________ Skill: Directions

DIRECTIONS:
Read each passage. Then, read the questions and answer choices. Mark the answer you have chosen. Mark the choice NH (not here) if the question cannot be answered from the information given.

Redecorate!

Want to give your bedroom a new look? It's as easy as grabbing a sponge and a bucket of paint! Painting the walls or ceiling in a room will give you a whole new look without spending a lot of money.

1. Decide which color you want for the base coat and which for the accent. The base coat will cover the entire wall while the accent is spotted over the base.
2. Purchase the paint, a paint roller if needed, and a sponge (natural sea sponges work better than man-made sponges).
3. Cover the floor with an old sheet or blanket to protect it from paint spills.
4. Use the roller to apply the base coat to the walls.
5. Let it dry for one day.
6. Dip the sponge in the accent color and squeeze out excess paint (until it is no longer dripping).
7. Lightly press the sponge onto the wall. Lift it directly off the wall all at one time (do not roll or push on the sponge).
8. Move your hand slightly and press again. Repeat this step until the color begins to fade and then redip your sponge.
9. Cover the entire wall with the accent color, or make geometric patterns. If you make a mistake, just sponge over it!

1. What do these directions help you to do?

   a make a painting
   b create a new look for walls with paint
   c redecorate the outside of your house
   d NH

2. How many colors of paint does this story recommend that you buy?

   f one
   g two
   h three
   j NH

3. With what should you apply the accent paint?

   a a paint roller
   b and old sheet or blanket
   c a natural sponge
   d NH

4. How much paint will you need to cover four walls in a bedroom?

   f 3 gallons
   g 2 quarts
   h 2 gallons
   j NH

5. What should you do after you apply the base coat to the walls?

   a apply the accent color
   b remove the sheet
   c let it dry for 24 hours
   d NH

6. What do you use to apply the base coat of paint?

   f a paint roller
   g and old sheet or blanket
   h a natural sponge
   j NH

Name ______________________ Skill: Charts and Graphs

DIRECTIONS:
Use the chart of graph to answer the questions. Mark the space for the answer you have chosen. Mark the choice NH (Not Here) if the question cannot be answered from the information given.

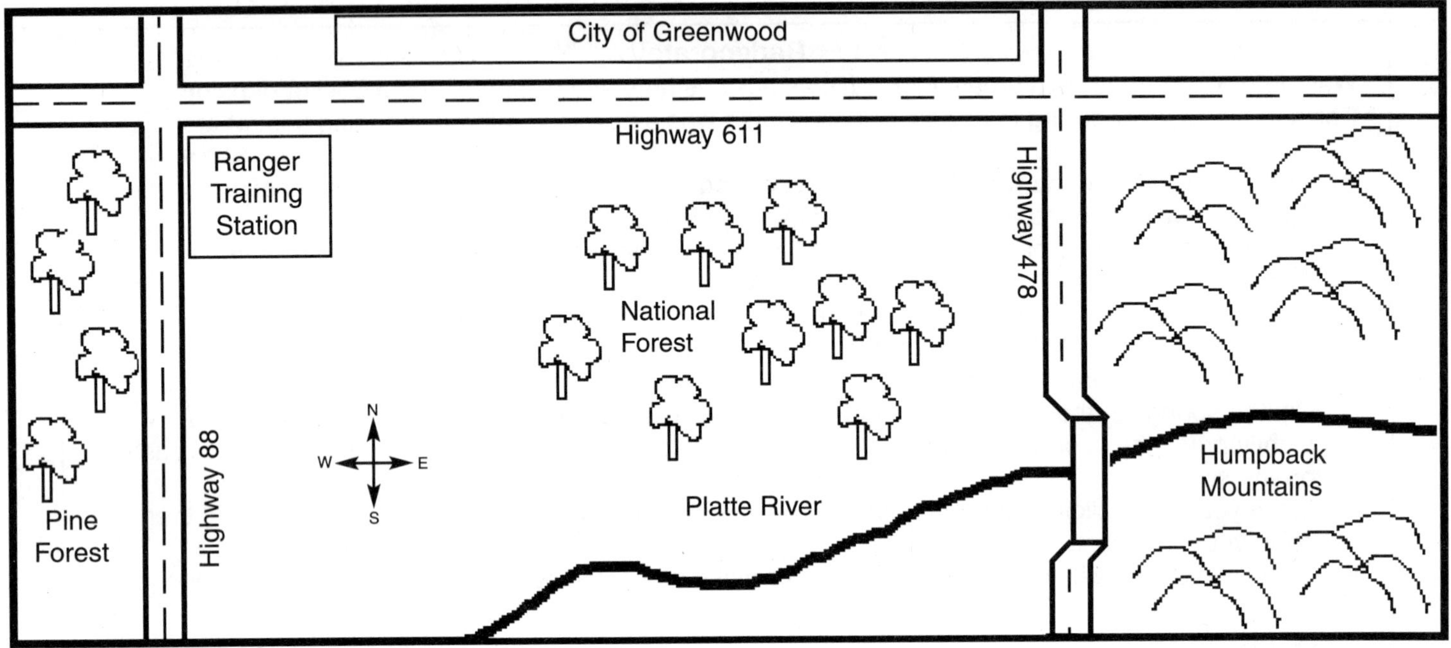

1. What is north of Highway 611?

   a National Forest
   b Greenwood
   c Humpback Mountains
   d NH

2. What crosses the Platte River?

   f Highway 88
   g Highway 478
   h Highway 611
   j NH

3. Which of these is closest to Highway 611?

   a Humpback Mountains
   b Platte River
   c National Forest
   d NH

4. National Forest is in which direction from Pine Forest?

   f west
   g east
   h northwest
   j NH

5. In which general directions does the Platte River run?

   a north and south
   b northwest and southeast
   c northeast and southwest
   d NH

6. What is east of Humpback Mountains?

   f National Forest
   g Greenwood
   h more mountains
   j NH

Name ______________________________ Skill: Charts and Graphs

DIRECTIONS:
Use the chart of graph to answer the questions. Mark the space for the answer you have chosen. Mark the choice NH (Not Here) if the question cannot be answered from the information given.

Tall Buildings

Building	Location	Height (in feet)	Stories Tall
Jin Mao Building	Shanghai, China	1,379	88
World Trade Center One	New York City	1,368	110
Empire State Building	New York City	1,250	102
T & C Tower	Kaoshung, Taiwan	1,140	85
John Hancock Center	Chicago	1,127	100
Chicago Beach Resort Hotel	Dubai, UAE	1,053	60
Baiyoke Tower	Bangkok, Thailand	1,050	90
Chrysler Building	New York City	1,046	77

1. What does this chart give us information about?

   a the tallest buildings in the world
   b tall building in America
   c tall buildings
   d NH

2. Which city on this chart has the most tall buildings?

   f Bangkok
   g Chicago
   h New York
   j NH

3. Which building listed has seventy-seven stories?

   a Empire State Building
   b Chrysler Building
   c First National Bank
   d NH

4. How tall is the tallest building on this chart?

   f 100 stories
   g 2,250 feet
   h 1,379 feet
   j NH

5. Which building has the least stories?

   a John Hancock Center
   b U.S. Steel Building
   c Chicago Beach Resort Hotel
   d NH

6. Which building was built in the shortest amount of time?

   f World Trade Center
   g Chrysler Building
   h Toronto Dominion Bank
   j NH

Name ______________________________ Skill: Charts and Graphs

DIRECTIONS:
Use the chart of graph to answer the questions. Mark the space for the answer you have chosen. Mark the choice NH (Not Here) if the question cannot be answered from the information given.

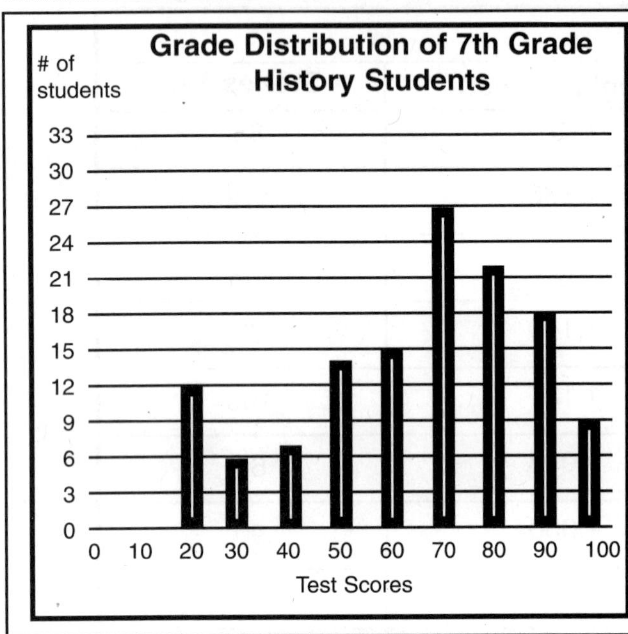

All 88 7th grade history students at Solomon Junior High took a semester exam. The teacher graphed the scores so the students could see the class results.

Class average = 68
Class average (all scores totalled then divided by the number of students taking the test)

Range = 80
Range is difference between top and bottom scores.

Mode = 70
Mode is the largest scoring group.

1. What information does the graph give us?

   a age of students in history
   b grades for 7th grade history test
   c test averages for 7th grade
   d NH

2. How many students scored a 90 on the test?

   f 18
   g 21
   h 22
   j NH

3. What does the word *mode* mean?

   a largest group of scores
   b spread of the scores
   c highest score achieved
   d NH

4. How many students took this exam?

   f 68
   g 80
   h 88
   j NH

5. How many students failed the exam?

   a 25
   b 37
   c 52
   d NH

6. How many students made the highest possible score?

   f 12
   g 9
   h 6
   j NH

Name ______________________ Skill: Charts and Graphs

DIRECTIONS:
Use the chart of graph to answer the questions. Mark the space for the answer you have chosen. Mark the choice NH (Not Here) if the question cannot be answered from the information given.

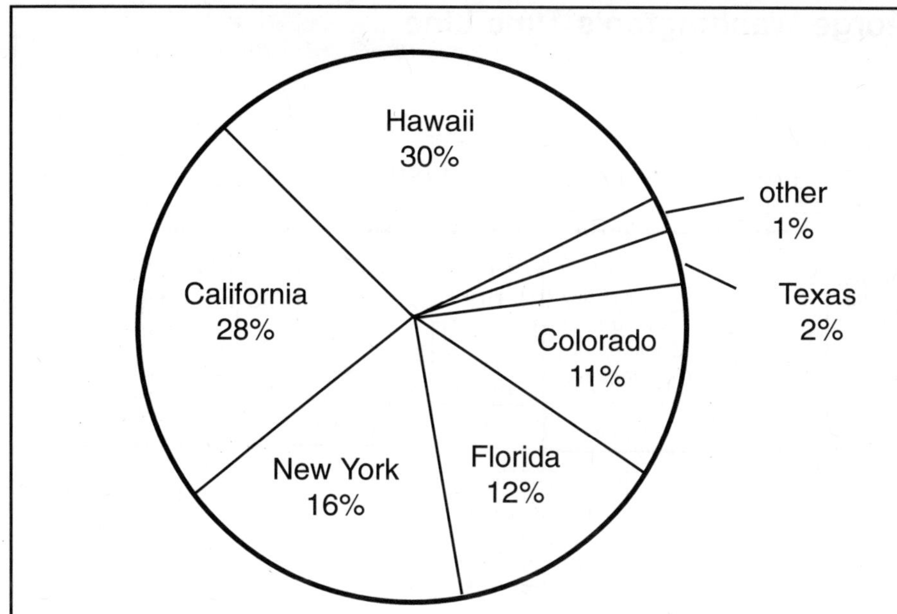

7th Graders Dream Vacation States

Over five thousand seventh grade students in schools across the country were asked which state they would most like to visit. This is how they responded.

1. What information does this pie graph give us?

   a what states people like
   b what vacations people like
   c what states 7th graders like
   d NH

2. Which states make up the category named "other"?

   f Louisiana, Michigan, Ohio
   g North Carolina and Wyoming
   h all of the other 44 states
   j NH

3. Which group has a larger percentage than Florida, but is less than California?

   a other
   b New York
   c Hawaii
   d NH

4. How many students were surveyed?

   f 100
   g all seventh graders
   h over 5000
   j NH

5. Which two states received 58% of the votes?

   a Colorado and Hawaii
   b California and Hawaii
   c New York and California
   d NH

6. How many groups have a smaller percentage than New York?

   f 6
   g 4
   h 2
   j NH

Name ______________________ Skill: Charts and Graphs

DIRECTIONS:
Use the chart of graph to answer the questions. Mark the space for the answer you have chosen. Mark the choice NH (Not Here) if the question cannot be answered from the information given.

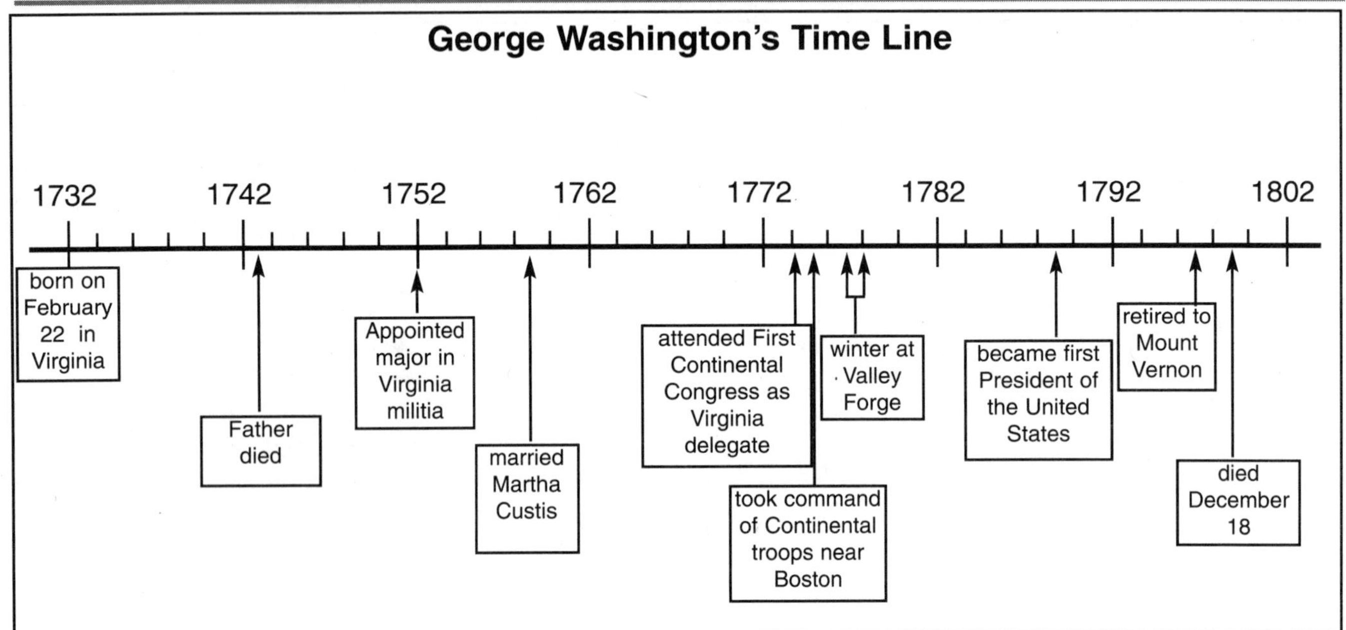

1. What information can you get from this chart?

   a main events in Washington's life
   b historical happenings in the world
   c Washington's favorite memories
   d NH

2. In what year did George Washington get married?

   f 1758
   g 1759
   h 1860
   j NH

3. How old was George when he became a major in the Virginia militia?

   a 20 years old
   b 27 years old
   c 30 years old
   d NH

4. What happened to Washington in 1789?

   f spent the winter at Valley Forge
   g became the President
   h retired
   j NH

5. In which year did Washington command near Boston?

   a 1772
   b 1773
   c 1775
   d NH

6. How old was Washington when he died?

   f 70 years old
   g 66 years old
   h 67 years old
   j NH

Name ______________________________ Skill: Charts and Graphs

DIRECTIONS:
Use the chart of graph to answer the questions. Mark the space for the answer you have chosen. Mark the choice NH (Not Here) if the question cannot be answered from the information given.

Planets in Our Solar System				
Planet	Distance from Sun	Rotation (Earth time)	Revolution	Named For
Mercury	57.9 million km.	59 Earth days	88 Earth days	Roman god
Venus	108.2 million km.	243 Earth days	225 Earth days	Roman goddess
Earth	149.6 million km.	23 hours 56 minutes	365.3 Earth days	Greek goddess Gaia
Mars	227.9 million km.	24 hours 37 minutes	687 Earth days	Roman god
Jupiter	778.3 million km.	9 hours 55 minutes	11.9 Earth years	Roman god
Saturn	1.4 billion km.	10 hours 40 minutes	29.5 Earth years	Roman god
Uranus	2.9 billion km.	17 hours 14 minutes	84 Earth years	Roman god
Neptune	4.5 billion km.	16 hours	165 Earth years	Roman god
Pluto	5.9 billion km.	6 Earth days 9 hours	248 Earth years	Roman god

1. What information can't you get from this table?

   a diameter of the planet
   b rotation
   c distance from the sun
   d NH

2. Which planets were named for goddesses?

   f Neptune and Mars
   g Venus and Pluto
   h Earth and Venus
   j NH

3. How long does it take for Mars to rotate once?

   a 23 hours 56 minutes
   b 24 hours 40 minutes
   c 11.9 Earth years
   d NH

4. Which planet takes 165 years to go just once around the sun?

   f Saturn
   g Neptune
   h Pluto
   j NH

5. Which planet has the warmest temperature?

   a Earth
   b Pluto
   c Saturn
   d NH

6. How many years does it take for Pluto to revolve around the sun just once?

   f 84 Earth years
   g 248 Earth years
   h 165 Earth years
   j NH

Name________________________________ Skill: Letters

DIRECTIONS:
Read each letter. Then, read each question and the answer choices. Mark the space for the answer you have chosen. Mark the choice NH (not here) if the question cannot be answered from the information given.

September 23, 1999

Dear *Prime* Magazine Editors,

I found your article on Justin Wallace to be really informative. I have been a fan of all his movies for the past several years, but I had no idea what the man was really like. I was pleased to find that Justin has two dogs and lets them both stay in the house. I understand what he means when he says that his dogs are his best friends. I am a dog lover as well. I have three beagles that sleep at the foot of my bed

I think it is admirable that Justin spends so much of his free time working to help the Society to Prevent Cruelty to Animals (SPCA). His generous spirit has inspired me to volunteer at the SPCA in my city. I find that working with the animals is very rewarding! Thanks for writing such an inspiring article.

A faithful reader,
Marla

1. To whom is this letter written?

   a Justin Wallace
   b the SPCA
   c magazine editors
   d NH

2. What did Marla enjoy finding out about Justin?

   f he likes dogs
   g he stars in movies
   h he inspires people
   j NH

3. What has Marla volunteered to do?

   a adopt more pets
   b write to Justin
   c work at the SPCA
   d NH

4. How many dogs does Marla own?

   f two
   g three
   h seven
   j NH

5. What word might best describe the type of person Justin is?

   a obedient
   b withdrawn
   c concerned
   d NH

6. What type of dogs does Justin own?

   f basset hounds
   g beagles
   h Irish setters
   j NH

Name________________________________ Skill: Letters

DIRECTIONS:
Read each letter. Then, read each question and the answer choices. Mark the space for the answer you have chosen. Mark the choice NH (not here) if the question cannot be answered from the information given.

October 1, 2000

Dear Mr. March,

I hope you are enjoying your new house. It must be nice now that you live so close to your grandchildren. I am happy for you, but I really miss having you live next door. The people who moved into your house are pretty nice, but I wish you still lived there.

I miss helping you in your garden and talking about the plants. My own garden did very well this summer. I remembered to put the fertilizer on, just as you told me, and my pumpkins are the biggest I have ever grown!

The pine tree you planted on the day your first grandson was born did not fare so well, I'm afraid. We had a big storm last week and the tree blew over in the wind. It didn't hit anything, but it cannot be replanted. I took three pine cones from the branches and am sending them to you. I thought you might like to start another tree from the seeds of this special one.

Happy growing!
Alexander Martin

1. What did Alexander grow in his garden this summer?
   - **a** pine trees
   - **b** pumpkins
   - **c** vegetables
   - **d** NH

2. What was special about the pine tree that blew down?
   - **f** Mr. March planted it for his grandson
   - **g** Mr. March planted it for his wife
   - **h** Alexander and Mr. March planted it
   - **j** NH

3. Where does Mr. March live?
   - **a** next door
   - **b** in another city
   - **c** in another state
   - **d** NH

4. What is Alexander sending to Mr. March?
   - **f** pumpkins
   - **g** fertilizer
   - **h** pine cones
   - **j** NH

5. What does Alexander miss about Mr. March?
   - **a** working together in the garden
   - **b** talking about the pine tree
   - **c** playing with his grandchildren
   - **d** NH

6. What are the new neighbors like?
   - **f** mean
   - **g** unfriendly
   - **h** nice
   - **j** NH

Name________________________________ Skill: Letters

DIRECTIONS:
Read each letter. Then, read each question and the answer choices. Mark the space for the answer you have chosen. Mark the choice NH (not here) if the question cannot be answered from the information given.

February 28, 1998

Dear Mrs. Burgess,

I read your advertisement in the newspaper and would like to apply for the position of nurse's assistant. I am seventeen years old and a junior at Westgate High School.Your ad said you need someone who is able to work afternoons and Saturdays. The hospital is very near my high school. I can walk there and be ready for work by 3:30 every week day. I can also be there by 8:00 every Saturday morning. I am dependable. I have been babysitting for the same three families for the past five years and have never once cancelled an engagement. I am a hard worker as well. I took over many of the household chores when I was fifteen and my mother became very ill. I learned a lot about nursing by watching how the visiting nurses would tend to my mother until she was well again. My hope is to go to college and someday be a nurse. In the mean time, I would like to learn as much as I can about the profession. I am sure you will find that I would be the perfect person for the job you are offering.

Sincerely,
Bonnie Bonutra

1. What is the purpose of this letter?

   a to say "thank you"
   b to share information
   c to ask for a job
   d NH

2. How did Bonnie find out about the job?

   f she heard about it at school
   g she read about it in the newspaper
   h her mother told her about it
   j NH

3. How does Bonnie support her statement that she is "dependable"?

   a she tells about her babysitting jobs
   b the school is close to the hospital
   c her mother has been very ill
   d NH

4. What is the job position Mrs. Burgess has open?

   f nurse
   g hospital aide
   h nurse's assistant
   j NH

5. What are the times that Mrs. Burgess needs a worker?

   a weekdays from noon to three
   b afternoons and evenings
   c afternoons and Saturdays
   d NH

6. How old is Bonnie?

   f 12
   g 15
   h 17
   j NH

Name________________________________ Skill: Letters

DIRECTIONS:
Read each letter. Then, read each question and the answer choices. Mark the space for the answer you have chosen. Mark the choice NH (not here) if the question cannot be answered from the information given.

May 8, 1999

Dear Mr. Grey,

Thank you for all the help you gave me with the social studies fair. I never realized how interesting it could be to make a project and do research. I know I sometimes don't listen well in your class and my test scores are never what they should be. It's just that I get a little distracted during class, and I find it is difficult to focus on the reading or on taking notes.

I never even thought about entering the social studies fair until you asked me what I was going to do for it. I really didn't think it would be something I would enjoy. Boy, was I wrong! Being able to choose my own topic was great. I have been interested in the culture of the Aztecs since my family went to Mexico three years ago. I like to read things about the Aztecs so it was the perfect choice for my project. The best part was that I got to ask a question and then do the research to find the answer! You sure made it a lot easier when you showed me how to use the computer to find all the answers I was looking for. Thank you so much!

From the runner up,
Robert Bailey

---

1. What is the purpose of this letter?

   a to say "thank you" to a teacher
   b to say "thank you" to a neighbor
   c to say "thank you" to a librarian
   d NH

2. How does Robert perform in social studies class?

   f he gets all A's
   g he doesn't try his hardest
   h he listens well but doesn't take notes
   j NH

3. What grade is Robert in at school?

   a 6th
   b 7th
   c 9th
   d NH

4. What was the topic of Robert's report?

   f using computers for research
   g culture in Mexico
   h Aztec culture
   j NH

5. Where did Robert get most of the information for his project?

   a from his teacher
   b from the library
   c from the computer
   d NH

6. How did Robert do at the Social Studies fair?

   f he won
   g he came in second place
   h he didn't win, but he learned a lot
   j NH

Name________________________________ Skill: Letters

DIRECTIONS:
Read each letter. Then, read each question and the answer choices. Mark the space for the answer you have chosen. Mark the choice NH (not here) if the question cannot be answered from the information given.

June 22, 2001

Dear John,

I had to go in to the office for an emergency meeting and probably won't be home until late this evening. I am sorry, but these things can't always be avoided. Please run to the grocery store and pick up a gallon of milk and a head of lettuce. I left twenty dollars on the kitchen counter under the car keys. You know I don't like for you to drive the car when I'm not home, but I will make an exception today. I asked Janice's mom to pick your sister up after school and take her to her dance lesson. The lesson is over at 5:00, and she will need a ride home. If you leave at 4:15 to get the groceries, you should be done shopping in plenty of time to pick up your sister. You two may order a pizza for dinner. Have it delivered and tell Mr. Penter to bill me for it. Don't forget to clean up the kitchen when you are done! I love you.

See you tonight!
Mom

1. Why did Mom leave this letter for John?
   - **a** to tell him to buy groceries
   - **b** to tell him he can drive the car now
   - **c** to give him information about what he needs to do
   - **d** NH

2. Where is John supposed to pick up his sister?
   - **f** at school
   - **g** at the dance lesson
   - **h** at Janice's house
   - **j** NH

3. Why isn't Mom home?
   - **a** she had to go to the dance lesson
   - **b** she had to go to the office
   - **c** she had an accident
   - **d** NH

4. What does John get to do that Mom usually won't let him do when she isn't home?
   - **f** drive the car
   - **g** order pizza
   - **h** buy groceries
   - **j** NH

5. How will John's sister get from school to the dance lesson?
   - **a** she'll take the bus
   - **b** John will drive her
   - **c** Janice's mom will take her
   - **d** NH

6. Where did Mom leave the car keys?
   - **f** in the car
   - **g** on the kitchen table
   - **h** on the counter
   - **j** NH

Name________________________________ Skill: Letters

DIRECTIONS:
Read each letter. Then, read each question and the answer choices. Mark the space for the answer you have chosen. Mark the choice NH (not here) if the question cannot be answered from the information given.

March 6, 1999

Dear Elly,

Roger and I just got back from my visit with Grandma and Grandpa. I like their new house in Florida. It is much smaller than the one they had in Michigan, but now that they are retired I guess they don't need as much space. I flew in on Tuesday and stayed until the next Monday. It was great because Roger and I got to miss a whole week of school! Thursday Gram and Gramps took us to Disney World. We had a blast! I liked riding the Skyway best of all. It was fun to be so high above everything, and I could see the whole park from there. Roger's favorite ride was the race cars. He said he wished they would go faster, but Gram thought they were too fast as it was! On Friday we went into an orange grove and got to pick our own grapefruit. That was a lot of fun, too. Saturday we drove to Tarpon Springs. Many people there make a living by diving for sponges. We took a tour on one of the boats, and it was really interesting. I can't wait to go back and visit again!

Your cousin,
Alyssa

---

1. What is the relationship between Elly and Alyssa?
   - **a** they are friends
   - **b** they are sisters
   - **c** they are cousins
   - **d** NH

2. Who is Roger?
   - **f** Alyssa's brother
   - **g** Elly's brother
   - **h** Alyssa's cousin
   - **j** NH

3. What did the children do on Friday?
   - **a** go to Disney World
   - **b** pick grapefruit
   - **c** visit Tarpon Springs
   - **d** NH

4. What did Roger think of the race car ride?
   - **f** fun, but it was too slow
   - **g** it was way too fast
   - **h** it was interesting
   - **j** NH

5. On what day did Alyssa see the sponge diver boats?
   - **a** Tuesday
   - **b** Thursday
   - **c** Saturday
   - **d** NH

6. On what day did Alyssa and Roger return home?
   - **f** Tuesday
   - **g** Sunday
   - **h** Monday
   - **j** NH

Name________________________________ Skill: Poetry

DIRECTIONS:
Read the poem. Then, read each question and the answer choices. Mark the space for the answer you have chosen. Mark the choice NH (not here) if the question cannot be answered from the information given.

A Boy
a traditional poem

A barefoot boy with shoes on
Came shuffling down the street,
His pants were full of pockets,
His shoes were full of feet.

He was born when just a baby,
His mother's pride and joy,
His only sister was a girl,
His brother was a boy.

He never was a triplet,
He never was a twin,
His legs were fastened to his knees
Just above the shin.

His teeth were fastened in his head
Several inches from his shoulder.
When he grew up he became a man
And every day grew older.

1. Which of these statements about this poem is true?
   a a girl is telling the story
   b twins are telling the story
   c a boy is telling the story
   d NH

2. Which line from the poem cannot possibly be true?
   f "His teeth were fastened in his head"
   g "He was born when just a baby"
   h "A barefoot boy with shoes on"
   j NH

3. What were the boy's pants full of?
   a shufflings
   b pockets
   c shoes
   d NH

4. What is the age of the boy in this poem?
   f just a baby
   g ten
   h a man
   j NH

5. How many siblings did the boy have?
   a one
   b two
   c three
   d NH

6. What does the poem tell you about the boy's legs?
   f they were a few inches from his shoulder
   g they were triplets
   h they were attached to his knees
   j NH

7. Which statement about the boy in this poem is true?
   a he became a man
   b he had a twin brother
   c he is a strange looking boy
   d NH

Name________________________________ Skill: Poetry

DIRECTIONS:
Read the poem. Then, read each question and the answer choices. Mark the space for the answer you have chosen. Mark the choice NH (not here) if the question cannot be answered from the information given.

End This Night

P. Pedigo

Day is dawning
Sun grows bright,
As the world
Turns from the night.

Birds are singing
Breeze does blow,
Night time creatures
Sleep below.

As the day
Starts bright and clear,
Those night time dreams
Will disappear.

1. What is happening in the first four lines?

   a the sun is rising
   b the sun is setting
   c the earth is warming
   d NH

2. What does "Night time creatures sleep below" most likely mean?

   f worms are under the soil
   g nocturnal animals have gone to bed
   h insects and bugs are sleeping
   j NH

3. What is the main idea of this poem?

   a animals sleep during the day
   b a new day is beginning
   c the earth rotates
   d NH

4. Which statement about this poem is true?

   f birds are sleeping in their nests
   g the stars are clear and bright
   h night is over
   j NH

5. Who is telling the story in this poem?

   a a boy
   b a woman
   c a child who had bad dreams
   d NH

6. What in this poem is "bright and clear"?

   f the stars
   g the breeze
   h the day
   j NH

7. What in this poem "grows bright"?

   a the sun
   b the night
   c the dreams
   d NH

Name________________________________ Skill: Poetry

DIRECTIONS:
Read the poem. Then, read each question and the answer choices. Mark the space for the answer you have chosen. Mark the choice NH (not here) if the question cannot be answered from the information given.

A Seasonal Poem
an adapted traditional poem

Spring:
Rain is showery,
Tulips are flowery,
Branches are bowery.

Summer:
Critters are lazy,
Heat makes us hazy,
Crops grow like crazy.

Autumn:
Allergies are wheezy,
Noses are sneezy,
Temperatures are freezy.

Winter:
Ice is slippy,
Snow is drippy,
Weather is nippy.

1. What is this poem about?
   - **a** spring flowers
   - **b** the heat of summer
   - **c** characteristics of each season
   - **d** NH

2. What is "nippy" in this poem?
   - **f** snow
   - **g** weather
   - **h** ice
   - **j** NH

3. According to the other clues about autumn, why are noses sneezy?
   - **a** people have colds or allergies
   - **b** the loose feathers tickle them
   - **c** there is too much pepper on the food
   - **d** NH

4. What does "Ice is slippy" mean?
   - **f** the ice is wet
   - **g** the ice is cold
   - **h** the ice is slippery
   - **j** NH

5. Which clue in the poem tells you the definition of the word "bowery"?
   - **a** showery
   - **b** flowery
   - **c** freezy
   - **d** NH

6. According to the poem, in which season do the crops grow?
   - **f** spring
   - **g** summer
   - **h** autumn
   - **j** NH

7. Using the winter clues of ice and snow, what do you suppose the "nippy" weather is?
   - **a** messy
   - **b** humid
   - **c** cold
   - **d** NH

Name________________________________ Skill: Poetry

DIRECTIONS:
Read the poem. Then, read each question and the answer choices. Mark the space for the answer you have chosen. Mark the choice NH (not here) if the question cannot be answered from the information given.

Two Runs To Win

A man on third, two batters out,
Two runs will win the game.
If I could hit a home run,
Great would be my fame.

I hitched up my pants,
Spit on my hands,
Pulled down my cap
And faced the howling stands.

"Ball three!" fans yelled with delight.
"Strike two!" the umpire said.
I knocked the next ball out of sight -
Then fell right out of bed.

1. What game is being referred to in this poem?
   - **a** football
   - **b** soccer
   - **c** baseball
   - **d** NH

2. How many outs did the team have when this person got up to bat?
   - **f** one
   - **g** two
   - **h** three
   - **j** NH

3. What would happen to this person if he hit a home run?
   - **a** his team would take the championship
   - **b** he would become famous
   - **c** he would be named player of the year
   - **d** NH

4. What did the teller of the poem do to his pants?
   - **f** spit on them
   - **g** pulled them down
   - **h** pulled them up
   - **j** NH

5. What does the teller of the poem do in the next to the last line?
   - **a** hit a home run
   - **b** strike out
   - **c** get another ball
   - **d** NH

6. What does the last line of this poem let you know?
   - **f** the person got a home run
   - **g** the person struck out
   - **h** the person was dreaming it all
   - **j** NH

7. What was the final score of this ball game?
   - **a** one to zero
   - **b** three to two
   - **c** two to two
   - **d** NH

Answer Key

Page 1

1 (a) (b) ● (d)
2 (f) ● (h) (j)
3 ● (b) (c) (d)
4 (f) (g) ● (j)
5 (a) (b) ● (d)
6 (f) ● (h) (j)
7 (a) (b) ● (d)
8 (f) ● (h) (j)
9 (a) (b) (c) ●
10 (f) ● (h) (j)

Page 2

1 (a) (b) ● (d)
2 (f) (g) ● (j)
3 (a) ● (c) (d)
4 (f) (g) (h) ●
5 (a) ● (c) (d)
6 (f) ● (h) (j)
7 (a) ● (c) (d)
8 (f) ● (h) (j)
9 (a) (b) ● (d)
10 (f) ● (h) (j)

Page 3

1 (a) (b) ● (d)
2 (f) (g) (h) ●
3 ● (b) (c) (d)
4 (f) ● (h) (j)
5 (a) (b) (c) ●
6 (f) (g) ● (j)
7 (a) ● (c) (d)
8 (f) (g) (h) ●
9 (a) (b) ● (d)
10 ● (g) (h) (j)

Page 4

1 ● (b) (c) (d)
2 (f) (g) (h) ●
3 (a) (b) ● (d)
4 (f) (g) (h) ●
5 (a) (b) ● (d)
6 (f) (g) ● (j)
7 (a) ● (c) (d)
8 ● (g) (h) (j)
9 (a) ● (c) (d)
10 (f) (g) ● (j)

Page 5

1 (a) (b) (c) ●
2 (f) (g) ● (j)
3 (a) (b) (c) ●
4 (f) (g) (h) ●
5 ● (b) (c) (d)
6 ● (g) (h) (j)
7 (a) (b) (c) ●
8 (f) ● (h) (j)
9 ● (b) (c) (d)
10 (f) (g) ● (j)

Page 6

1 ● (b) (c) (d)
2 (f) ● (h) (j)
3 (a) ● (c) (d)
4 (f) (g) ● (j)
5 (a) (b) (c) ●
6 (f) (g) ● (j)
7 (a) ● (c) (d)
8 (f) ● (h) (j)
9 (a) (b) ● (d)
10 (f) (g) ● (j)

Page 7

1 ● (b) (c) (d)
2 ● (g) (h) (j)
3 ● (b) (c) (d)
4 (f) ● (h) (j)
5 (a) ● (c) (d)
6 (f) (g) (h) ●
7 (a) (b) (c) ●
8 (f) ● (h) (j)
9 (a) (b) ● (d)
10 ● (g) (h) (j)

Page 8

1 (a) (b) ● (d)
2 (f) ● (h) (j)
3 (a) (b) ● (d)
4 (f) ● (h) (j)
5 ● (b) (c) (d)
6 (f) (g) (h) ●
7 ● (b) (c) (d)
8 (f) ● (h) (j)
9 (a) (b) ● (d)
10 (f) ● (h) (j)
11 (a) (b) (c) ●
12 ● (g) (h) (j)
13 (a) (b) (c) ●
14 ● (g) (h) (j)
15 (a) ● (c) (d)
16 (f) (g) ● (j)
17 (a) ● (c) (d)
18 (f) (g) ● (j)

Page 9

1 (a) (b) ● (d)
2 (f) (g) ● (j)
3 (a) (b) ● (d)
4 (f) ● (h) (j)
5 ● (b) (c) (d)
6 (f) (g) (h) ●
7 (a) (b) (c) ●
8 ● (g) (h) (j)
9 (a) ● (c) (d)
10 ● (g) (h) (j)
11 (a) (b) ● (d)
12 (f) ● (h) (j)
13 ● (b) (c) (d)
14 (f) ● (h) (j)
15 (a) (b) (c) ●
16 (f) (g) (h) ●
17 (a) ● (c) (d)
18 (f) (g) (h) ●

Page 10

1 (a) ● (c) (d)
2 (f) (g) (h) ●
3 ● (b) (c) (d)
4 ● (g) (h) (j)
5 (a) ● (c) (d)
6 (f) ● (h) (j)
7 (a) (b) ● (d)
8 ● (g) (h) (j)
9 ● (b) (c) (d)
10 (f) (g) (h) ●
11 ● (b) (c) (d)
12 (f) (g) ● (j)
13 (a) ● (c) (d)
14 (f) ● (h) (j)
15 (a) (b) ● (d)
16 ● (g) (h) (j)
17 (a) (b) ● (d)
18 (f) (g) (h) ●

Page 11

1 ● (b) (c) (d)
2 (f) (g) ● (j)
3 (a) (b) ● (d)
4 ● (g) (h) (j)
5 (a) (b) ● (d)
6 (f) ● (h) (j)
7 (a) ● (c) (d)
8 (f) (g) ● (j)
9 ● (b) (c) (d)
10 (f) (g) (h) ●
11 (a) ● (c) (d)
12 ● (g) (h) (j)
13 (a) (b) ● (d)
14 (f) (g) ● (j)
15 (a) (b) (c) ●
16 (f) (g) ● (j)
17 ● (b) (c) (d)
18 (f) ● (h) (j)

Page 12

1 (a) ● (c) (d)
2 (f) (g) (h) ●
3 (a) (b) (c) ●
4 (f) (g) ● (j)
5 (a) (b) (c) ●
6 (f) ● (h) (j)
7 ● (b) (c) (d)
8 (f) (g) ● (j)
9 ● (b) (c) (d)
10 (f) (g) (h) ●
11 (a) ● (c) (d)
12 (f) ● (h) (j)
13 (a) (b) ● (d)
14 (f) ● (h) (j)
15 (a) (b) ● (d)
16 ● (g) (h) (j)
17 ● (b) (c) (d)
18 (f) (g) (h) ●

Answer Key

Page 13

1	a	b	c	●
2	f	g	h	●
3	●	b	c	d
4	f	●	h	j
5	a	●	c	d
6	f	g	●	j
7	a	●	c	d
8	f	g	●	j
9	a	●	c	d
10	f	g	h	●
11	●	b	c	d
12	●	g	h	j
13	a	b	●	d
14	f	●	h	j
15	a	b	●	d
16	f	g	●	j
17	a	b	c	●
18	●	g	h	j

Page 14

1	a	●	c	d
2	f	g	●	j
3	a	b	c	●
4	f	g	h	●
5	●	b	c	d
6	●	g	h	j
7	a	●	c	d
8	●	g	h	j
9	a	●	c	d
10	f	g	h	●
11	a	b	●	d
12	f	●	h	j
13	a	●	c	d
14	f	g	h	●
15	a	b	●	d
16	f	g	●	j
17	a	b	●	d
18	●	g	h	j

Page 15

1	a	b	●	d
2	f	●	h	j
3	a	b	●	d
4	●	g	h	j
5	a	b	c	●
6	f	●	h	j
7	a	b	c	●
8	f	g	h	●
9	●	b	c	d
10	f	g	h	●
11	●	b	c	d
12	f	g	●	j
13	●	b	c	d
14	f	g	h	●
15	a	●	c	d
16	f	g	h	●
17	a	b	●	d
18	f	g	●	j

Page 16

1	a	b	●	d
2	f	g	h	●
3	a	●	c	d
4	f	g	●	j
5	a	●	c	d
6	f	●	h	j
7	a	●	c	d
8	f	g	h	●
9	a	b	●	d
10	●	g	h	j
11	a	b	c	●
12	●	g	h	j
13	●	b	c	d
14	f	g	●	j
15	●	b	c	d
16	f	●	h	j
17	a	b	c	●
18	f	●	h	j

Page 17

1	a	b	●	d
2	f	g	h	●
3	●	b	c	d
4	●	g	h	j
5	●	b	c	d
6	●	g	h	j
7	a	b	●	d
8	f	g	h	●
9	●	b	c	d
10	f	g	h	●
11	a	b	●	d
12	f	g	h	●
13	●	b	c	d
14	●	g	h	j
15	a	b	c	●
16	f	g	h	●
17	a	●	c	d
18	●	g	h	j

Page 18

1	a	b	●	d
2	f	●	h	j
3	●	b	c	d
4	f	●	h	j
5	a	b	c	●
6	f	g	h	●
7	a	●	c	d
8	f	g	h	●
9	●	b	c	d
10	f	g	h	●
11	a	b	c	●
12	f	g	●	j
13	a	b	●	d
14	f	g	h	●
15	a	b	●	d
16	f	●	h	j
17	●	b	c	d
18	f	g	●	j

Page 19

1	a	b	c	●
2	●	g	h	j
3	a	●	c	d
4	●	g	h	j
5	a	b	c	●
6	f	g	●	j
7	a	●	c	d
8	●	g	h	j
9	a	●	c	d
10	f	●	h	j
11	a	b	c	●
12	f	●	h	j
13	a	●	c	d
14	●	g	h	j
15	a	b	●	d
16	f	g	●	j
17	a	●	c	d
18	f	g	h	●

Page 20

1	a	b	●	d
2	●	g	h	j
3	a	b	c	●
4	f	g	●	j
5	a	b	c	●
6	●	g	h	j
7	a	●	c	d
8	f	g	●	j
9	a	●	c	d
10	f	●	h	j
11	●	b	c	d
12	f	●	h	j
13	●	b	c	d
14	f	g	●	j
15	a	b	c	●
16	●	g	h	j
17	a	●	c	d
18	f	●	h	j

Page 21

1	●	b	c	d
2	f	●	h	j
3	a	b	c	●
4	●	g	h	j
5	a	b	c	●
6	f	g	h	●
7	a	b	c	●
8	●	g	h	j
9	a	●	c	d
10	●	g	h	j
11	a	●	c	d
12	f	g	●	j
13	a	b	c	●
14	f	●	h	j
15	a	b	●	d
16	f	●	h	j
17	●	b	c	d
18	f	g	●	j

Page 22

1	a	b	●	d
2	f	●	h	j
3	a	●	c	d
4	●	g	h	j
5	●	b	c	d
6	f	g	h	●
7	●	b	c	d
8	f	g	●	j
9	a	b	c	●
10	f	●	h	j

Page 23

1	a	b	c	●
2	f	g	h	●
3	a	b	●	d
4	f	g	●	j
5	a	●	c	d
6	f	g	●	j
7	a	●	c	d
8	●	g	h	j
9	a	●	c	d
10	f	g	●	j

Page 24

1	a	b	●	d
2	f	g	●	j
3	a	b	●	d
4	f	g	●	j
5	a	●	c	d
6	f	g	●	j
7	●	b	c	d
8	f	g	●	j
9	a	b	c	●
10	●	g	h	j

Page 25

1	a	●	c	d
2	f	g	h	●
3	a	●	c	d
4	f	g	●	j
5	a	●	c	d
6	f	g	●	j
7	a	●	c	d
8	f	g	●	j
9	a	b	c	●
10	f	g	●	j

Page 26

1	●	b	c	d
2	f	●	h	j
3	a	b	c	●
4	f	g	●	j
5	●	b	c	d
6	f	g	●	j
7	a	b	●	d
8	●	g	h	j
9	a	b	c	●
10	f	●	h	j

Page 27

1	a	●	c	d
2	f	g	h	●
3	a	b	●	d
4	f	●	h	j
5	a	b	●	d
6	f	g	●	j
7	a	●	c	d
8	●	g	h	j
9	a	●	c	d
10	●	g	h	j

Answer Key

	Page 28	Page 29	Page 30	Page 31	Page 32	Page 33
1	● b c d	a ● c d	● b c d	a b ● d	a b c ●	a b ● d
2	f g ● j	f g h ●	f g ● j	● g h j	f ● h j	● g h j
3	a b c ●	● b c d	a ● c d	a b ● d	● b c d	● b c d
4	f ● h j	f ● h j	● g h j	● g h j	f g ● j	f g h ●
5	a b c ●	● b c d	● b c d	a ● c d	● b c d	a ● c d
6	f g ● j	f g h ●	f g ● j	f g h ●	f ● h j	f ● h j
7	a b c ●	a ● c d	● b c d	a ● c d	a ● c d	a b c ●
8	f ● h j	● g h j	f ● h j	f g ● j	● g h j	f g ● j
9	● b c d	a b c ●	a b c ●	a b c ●	a b c ●	● b c d
10	f g ● j	f ● h j	● g h j	f g ● j	f g ● j	f g ● j

	Page 34	Page 35	Page 36	Page 37	Page 38	Page 39
1	● b c d	● b c d	● b c d	a b ● d	a ● c d	a ● c d
2	f g ● j	● g h j	● g h j	f g ● j	f g ● j	f g h ●
3	● b c d	a b ● d	a b ● d	● b c d	a b c ●	a ● c d
4	f g h ●	f g h ●	f g h ●	f g ● j	f ● h j	f g ● j
5	a ● c d	a b ● d	a ● c d	● b c d	a ● c d	a ● c d
6	f g h ●	f g ● j	● g h j	f ● h j	f ● h j	f g h ●
7	● b c d	a b c ●	● b c d	a b ● d	a b ● d	a b c ●
8	f ● h j	f ● h j	f ● h j	● g h j	f g h ●	f g ● j
9	a ● c d	● b c d	a ● c d	a b c ●	● b c d	a ● c d
10	f g h ●	f g ● j	f g ● j	f g h ●	f g ● j	● g h j

	Page 40	Page 41	Page 42	Page 43	Page 44	Page 45
1	a b c ●	● b c d	a ● c d	● b c d	a b ● d	a b ● d
2	f ● h j	● g h j	● g h j	f g h ●	f g ● j	● g h j
3	a ● c d	a ● c d	a ● c d	a ● c d	● b c d	a b ● d
4	f g h ●	f g ● j	f g ● j	f g ● j	f g h ●	f g h ●
5	a b ● d	a b c ●	a b ● d	a ● c d	a b c ●	a b ● d
6	● g h j	f g ● j	f ● h j	f g ● j	● g h j	f g h ●
7	a b ● d	a b c ●	● b c d	● b c d	● b c d	● b c d
8	f ● h j	f g ● j	f g ● j	f g ● j	● g h j	● g h j
9	a b ● d	a b ● d	a b c ●	a b c ●	● b c d	● b c d
10	f ● h j	f ● h j	f ● h j	f ● h j	f g h ●	f g ● j

Answer Key

Page 46

1 ⓐ ⓑ ● ⓓ
2 ⓕ ⓖ ● ⓙ
3 ● ⓑ ⓒ ⓓ
4 ⓕ ⓖ ⓗ ●
5 ⓐ ⓑ ● ⓓ
6 ⓕ ⓖ ⓗ ●
7 ● ⓑ ⓒ ⓓ
8 ⓕ ⓖ ⓗ ●
9 ⓐ ⓑ ⓒ ●
10 ⓕ ⓖ ● ⓙ

Page 47

1 ● ⓑ ⓒ ⓓ
2 ⓕ ● ⓗ ⓙ
3 ⓐ ⓑ ⓒ ●
4 ⓕ ⓖ ● ⓙ
5 ⓐ ● ⓒ ⓓ
6 ⓕ ⓖ ● ⓙ
7 ⓐ ⓑ ⓒ ●
8 ● ⓖ ⓗ ⓙ
9 ⓐ ⓑ ● ⓓ
10 ⓕ ⓖ ⓗ ●

Page 48

1 ⓐ ⓑ ● ⓓ
2 ⓕ ⓖ ● ⓙ
3 ⓐ ● ⓒ ⓓ
4 ⓕ ⓖ ● ⓙ
5 ● ⓑ ⓒ ⓓ
6 ⓕ ● ⓗ ⓙ
7 ⓐ ⓑ ● ⓓ
8 ⓕ ⓖ ● ⓙ
9 ⓐ ⓑ ⓒ ●
10 ⓕ ⓖ ● ⓙ

Page 49

1 ⓐ ⓑ ● ⓓ
2 ● ⓖ ⓗ ⓙ
3 ⓐ ⓑ ⓒ ●
4 ⓕ ● ⓗ ⓙ
5 ● ⓑ ⓒ ⓓ
6 ⓕ ● ⓗ ⓙ
7 ⓐ ⓑ ● ⓓ
8 ⓕ ⓖ ● ⓙ
9 ⓐ ⓑ ⓒ ●
10 ⓕ ⓖ ● ⓙ

Page 50

1 ⓐ ⓑ ● ⓓ
2 ⓕ ⓖ ⓗ ●
3 ● ⓑ ⓒ ⓓ
4 ⓕ ● ⓗ ⓙ
5 ⓐ ● ⓒ ⓓ
6 ⓕ ⓖ ● ⓙ
7 ⓐ ⓑ ⓒ ●
8 ⓕ ⓖ ● ⓙ
9 ⓐ ⓑ ⓒ ●
10 ● ⓖ ⓗ ⓙ

Page 51

1 ⓐ ⓑ ● ⓓ
2 ⓕ ⓖ ⓗ ●
3 ● ⓑ ⓒ ⓓ
4 ⓕ ● ⓗ ⓙ
5 ⓐ ⓑ ● ⓓ
6 ● ⓖ ⓗ ⓙ
7 ⓐ ⓑ ● ⓓ
8 ⓕ ● ⓗ ⓙ
9 ⓐ ⓑ ● ⓓ
10 ⓕ ⓖ ● ⓙ

Page 52

1 ⓐ ● ⓒ ⓓ
2 ⓕ ⓖ ⓗ ●
3 ⓐ ● ⓒ ⓓ
4 ● ⓖ ⓗ ⓙ
5 ⓐ ⓑ ● ⓓ
6 ⓕ ⓖ ⓗ ●
7 ● ⓑ ⓒ ⓓ
8 ⓕ ⓖ ⓗ ●
9 ● ⓑ ⓒ ⓓ
10 ⓕ ⓖ ⓗ ●

Page 53

1 ⓐ ⓑ ⓒ ●
2 ● ⓖ ⓗ ⓙ
3 ⓐ ⓑ ● ⓓ
4 ● ⓖ ⓗ ⓙ
5 ⓐ ⓑ ● ⓓ
6 ⓕ ⓖ ● ⓙ
7 ⓐ ● ⓒ ⓓ
8 ⓕ ⓖ ● ⓙ
9 ⓐ ● ⓒ ⓓ
10 ● ⓖ ⓗ ⓙ

Page 54

1 ⓐ ⓑ ⓒ ●
2 ⓕ ⓖ ⓗ ●
3 ⓐ ● ⓒ ⓓ
4 ⓕ ⓖ ⓗ ●
5 ⓐ ⓑ ● ⓓ
6 ● ⓖ ⓗ ⓙ
7 ⓐ ● ⓒ ⓓ
8 ● ⓖ ⓗ ⓙ
9 ⓐ ● ⓒ ⓓ
10 ⓕ ⓖ ● ⓙ

Page 55

1 ⓐ ⓑ ⓒ ●
2 ⓕ ⓖ ● ⓙ
3 ⓐ ⓑ ⓒ ●
4 ⓕ ● ⓗ ⓙ
5 ⓐ ⓑ ⓒ ●
6 ⓕ ● ⓗ ⓙ
7 ⓐ ⓑ ⓒ ●
8 ⓕ ⓖ ⓗ ●
9 ⓐ ⓑ ⓒ ●
10 ⓕ ⓖ ● ⓙ

Page 56

1 ● ⓑ ⓒ ⓓ
2 ⓕ ● ⓗ ⓙ
3 ⓐ ● ⓒ ⓓ
4 ● ⓖ ⓗ ⓙ
5 ⓐ ● ⓒ ⓓ
6 ⓕ ⓖ ⓗ ●

Page 57

1 ⓐ ⓑ ● ⓓ
2 ⓕ ● ⓗ ⓙ
3 ● ⓑ ⓒ ⓓ
4 ⓕ ⓖ ● ⓙ
5 ⓐ ⓑ ● ⓓ
6 ⓕ ⓖ ⓗ ●

Page 58

1 ⓐ ● ⓒ ⓓ
2 ⓕ ● ⓗ ⓙ
3 ⓐ ● ⓒ ⓓ
4 ⓕ ● ⓗ ⓙ
5 ● ⓑ ⓒ ⓓ
6 ⓕ ⓖ ⓗ ●

Page 59

1 ⓐ ⓑ ● ⓓ
2 ● ⓖ ⓗ ⓙ
3 ⓐ ● ⓒ ⓓ
4 ⓕ ⓖ ● ⓙ
5 ⓐ ● ⓒ ⓓ

Page 60

1 ⓐ ⓑ ● ⓓ
2 ⓕ ● ⓗ ⓙ
3 ● ⓑ ⓒ ⓓ
4 ⓕ ⓖ ● ⓙ
5 ⓐ ● ⓒ ⓓ

Page 61

1 ⓐ ● ⓒ ⓓ
2 ⓕ ● ⓗ ⓙ
3 ● ⓑ ⓒ ⓓ
4 ⓕ ⓖ ● ⓙ
5 ● ⓑ ⓒ ⓓ

Page 62

1 ⓐ ● ⓒ ⓓ
2 ⓕ ⓖ ● ⓙ
3 ⓐ ● ⓒ ⓓ
4 ⓕ ⓖ ● ⓙ
5 ⓐ ⓑ ⓒ ●

Page 63

1 ⓐ ⓑ ● ⓓ
2 ● ⓖ ⓗ ⓙ
3 ⓐ ● ⓒ ⓓ
4 ⓕ ⓖ ● ⓙ
5 ⓐ ● ⓒ ⓓ

Page 64

1 ⓐ ⓑ ● ⓓ
2 ⓕ ● ⓗ ⓙ
3 ⓐ ⓑ ● ⓓ
4 ⓕ ⓖ ● ⓙ
5 ⓐ ⓑ ● ⓓ

Page 65

1 ⓐ ● ⓒ ⓓ
2 ● ⓖ ⓗ ⓙ
3 ⓐ ⓑ ● ⓓ
4 ● ⓖ ⓗ ⓙ
5 ⓐ ⓑ ⓒ ●
6 ⓕ ⓖ ● ⓙ

Page 66

1 ⓐ ⓑ ● ⓓ
2 ⓕ ⓖ ● ⓙ
3 ⓐ ⓑ ● ⓓ
4 ● ⓖ ⓗ ⓙ
5 ⓐ ⓑ ⓒ ●

Page 67

1 ⓐ ⓑ ● ⓓ
2 ⓕ ⓖ ● ⓙ
3 ⓐ ● ⓒ ⓓ
4 ⓕ ⓖ ⓗ ●
5 ⓐ ⓑ ● ⓓ

Page 68

1 ⓐ ⓑ ● ⓓ
2 ● ⓖ ⓗ ⓙ
3 ⓐ ● ⓒ ⓓ
4 ⓕ ⓖ ● ⓙ
5 ● ⓑ ⓒ ⓓ
6 ⓕ ⓖ ⓗ ●

Page 69

1 ⓐ ⓑ ● ⓓ
2 ⓕ ● ⓗ ⓙ
3 ⓐ ⓑ ● ⓓ
4 ● ⓖ ⓗ ⓙ
5 ⓐ ⓑ ⓒ ●

Answer Key

Page 70	Page 71	Page 72	Page 73	Page 74	Page 75
1 ● b c d	1 a b ● d	1 a b ● d	1 ● b c d	1 a b ● d	1 a ● c d
2 f g ● j	2 ● g h j	2 f ● h j	2 f ● h j	2 f ● h j	2 f g ● j
3 a ● c d	3 a b ● d	3 a b ● d	3 a b ● d	3 a b ● d	3 ● b c d
4 f g ● j	4 f g ● j	4 ● g h j	4 f g h ●	4 f g h ●	4 f ● h j
5 a b ● d	5 a ● c d	5 a b ● d	5 a ● c d	5 a b ● d	5 a b c ●

Page 76	Page 77	Page 78	Page 79	Page 80	Page 81
1 a ● c d	1 a ● c d	1 a b ● d	1 a ● c d	1 a b ● d	1 a b ● d
2 f ● h j	2 f ● h j	2 f ● h j	2 f g ● j	2 f g ● j	2 f g ● j
3 a ● c d	3 a ● c d	3 ● b c d	3 ● b c d	3 a ● c d	3 a ● c d
4 ● g h j	4 f g ● j	4 f g h ●	4 f g ● j	4 ● g h j	4 f g h ●
5 a ● c d	5 ● b c d	5 a b ● d	5 a b ● d	5 a b ● d	5 a b ● d
	6 f g h ●	6 ● g h j			

Page 82	Page 83	Page 84	Page 85	Page 86	Page 87
1 a ● c d	1 a ● c d	1 a ● c d	1 a b ● d	1 a b ● d	1 a b ● d
2 ● g h j	2 f g ● j	2 ● g h j	2 f g h ●	2 f g ● j	2 ● g h j
3 a b ● d	3 a b ● d	3 a b ● d	3 a b c ●	3 a b ● d	3 a b ● d
4 f ● h j	4 ● g h j	4 f g ● j	4 f ● h j	4 f g ● j	4 f ● h j
5 a b c ●	5 ● b c d	5 a b ● d	5 a ● c d	5 a b ● d	5 a b c ●
	6 ● g h j	6 f g ● j	6 f ● h j	6 f g h ●	6 f g ● j

Page 88	Page 89	Page 90	Page 91	Page 92	Page 93
1 a ● c d	1 a ● c d	1 a b ● d	1 a ● c d	1 a b ● d	1 ● b c d
2 f ● h j	2 f g ● j	2 f g ● j	2 ● g h j	2 f g h ●	2 f ● h j
3 a b ● d	3 ● b c d	3 a ● c d	3 ● b c d	3 a ● c d	3 ● b c d
4 f g h ●	4 f ● h j	4 f g ● j	4 f g ● j	4 f g ● j	4 f ● h j
5 a b ● d	5 a b ● d	5 a b ● d	5 a b c ●	5 a ● c d	5 a b ● d
6 ● g h j	6 f g h ●	6 f g h ●	6 f ● h j	6 f ● h j	6 f g ● j

Page 94	Page 95	Page 96	Page 97	Page 98	Page 99
1 ● b c d	1 a b ● d	1 a ● c d	1 a b ● d	1 ● b c d	1 a b ● d
2 f g ● j	2 ● g h j	2 ● g h j	2 f ● h j	2 f ● h j	2 f ● h j
3 a ● c d	3 a b ● d	3 a b c ●	3 ● b c d	3 a b c ●	3 a ● c d
4 f ● h j	4 f ● h j	4 f g ● j	4 f g ● j	4 f g ● j	4 ● g h j
5 a b c ●	5 a b ● d	5 ● b c d	5 a b ● d	5 a b ● d	5 a b ● d
6 f ● h j	6 f g h ●	6 f g ● j	6 f g ● j	6 f ● h j	6 f g ● j

Answer Key

Page 100	Page 101	Page 102	Page 103	Page 104
1 ⓐ ⓑ ● ⓓ	1 ⓐ ⓑ ⓒ ●	1 ● ⓑ ⓒ ⓓ	1 ⓐ ⓑ ● ⓓ	1 ⓐ ⓑ ● ⓓ
2 ⓕ ⓖ ⓗ ●	2 ⓕ ⓖ ● ⓙ	2 ⓕ ● ⓗ ⓙ	2 ⓕ ● ⓗ ⓙ	2 ⓕ ● ⓗ ⓙ
3 ⓐ ● ⓒ ⓓ	3 ⓐ ● ⓒ ⓓ	3 ⓐ ● ⓒ ⓓ	3 ● ⓑ ⓒ ⓓ	3 ⓐ ● ⓒ ⓓ
4 ● ⓖ ⓗ ⓙ	4 ⓕ ⓖ ⓗ ●	4 ⓕ ⓖ ● ⓙ	4 ⓕ ⓖ ● ⓙ	4 ⓕ ⓖ ● ⓙ
5 ⓐ ⓑ ● ⓓ	5 ⓐ ● ⓒ ⓓ	5 ⓐ ⓑ ⓒ ●	5 ⓐ ⓑ ⓒ ●	5 ● ⓑ ⓒ ⓓ
6 ⓕ ⓖ ● ⓙ	6 ⓕ ⓖ ● ⓙ	6 ⓕ ⓖ ● ⓙ	6 ⓕ ● ⓗ ⓙ	6 ⓕ ⓖ ● ⓙ
	7 ● ⓑ ⓒ ⓓ	7 ● ⓑ ⓒ ⓓ	7 ⓐ ⓑ ● ⓓ	7 ⓐ ⓑ ⓒ ●

Name________________________________ **Answer Sheet-Word Skills**

Analogies page_____	Syllables page_____	Spelling page_____	Synonyms page_____	Homophones page_____	Vocabulary page_____
1 ⓐ ⓑ ⓒ ⓓ	1 ⓐ ⓑ ⓒ ⓓ	1 ⓐ ⓑ ⓒ ⓓ	1 ⓐ ⓑ ⓒ ⓓ	1 ⓐ ⓑ ⓒ ⓓ	1 ⓐ ⓑ ⓒ ⓓ
2 ⓕ ⓖ ⓗ ⓙ	2 ⓕ ⓖ ⓗ ⓙ	2 ⓕ ⓖ ⓗ ⓙ	2 ⓕ ⓖ ⓗ ⓙ	2 ⓕ ⓖ ⓗ ⓙ	2 ⓕ ⓖ ⓗ ⓙ
3 ⓐ ⓑ ⓒ ⓓ	3 ⓐ ⓑ ⓒ ⓓ	3 ⓐ ⓑ ⓒ ⓓ	3 ⓐ ⓑ ⓒ ⓓ	3 ⓐ ⓑ ⓒ ⓓ	3 ⓐ ⓑ ⓒ ⓓ
4 ⓕ ⓖ ⓗ ⓙ	4 ⓕ ⓖ ⓗ ⓙ	4 ⓕ ⓖ ⓗ ⓙ	4 ⓕ ⓖ ⓗ ⓙ	4 ⓕ ⓖ ⓗ ⓙ	4 ⓕ ⓖ ⓗ ⓙ
5 ⓐ ⓑ ⓒ ⓓ	5 ⓐ ⓑ ⓒ ⓓ	5 ⓐ ⓑ ⓒ ⓓ	5 ⓐ ⓑ ⓒ ⓓ	5 ⓐ ⓑ ⓒ ⓓ	5 ⓐ ⓑ ⓒ ⓓ
6 ⓕ ⓖ ⓗ ⓙ	6 ⓕ ⓖ ⓗ ⓙ	6 ⓕ ⓖ ⓗ ⓙ	6 ⓕ ⓖ ⓗ ⓙ	6 ⓕ ⓖ ⓗ ⓙ	6 ⓕ ⓖ ⓗ ⓙ
7 ⓐ ⓑ ⓒ ⓓ	7 ⓐ ⓑ ⓒ ⓓ	7 ⓐ ⓑ ⓒ ⓓ	7 ⓐ ⓑ ⓒ ⓓ	7 ⓐ ⓑ ⓒ ⓓ	7 ⓐ ⓑ ⓒ ⓓ
8 ⓕ ⓖ ⓗ ⓙ	8 ⓕ ⓖ ⓗ ⓙ	8 ⓕ ⓖ ⓗ ⓙ	8 ⓕ ⓖ ⓗ ⓙ	8 ⓕ ⓖ ⓗ ⓙ	8 ⓕ ⓖ ⓗ ⓙ
9 ⓐ ⓑ ⓒ ⓓ	9 ⓐ ⓑ ⓒ ⓓ	9 ⓐ ⓑ ⓒ ⓓ	9 ⓐ ⓑ ⓒ ⓓ	9 ⓐ ⓑ ⓒ ⓓ	9 ⓐ ⓑ ⓒ ⓓ
10 ⓕ ⓖ ⓗ ⓙ	10 ⓕ ⓖ ⓗ ⓙ	10 ⓕ ⓖ ⓗ ⓙ	10 ⓕ ⓖ ⓗ ⓙ	10 ⓕ ⓖ ⓗ ⓙ	10 ⓕ ⓖ ⓗ ⓙ
	11 ⓐ ⓑ ⓒ ⓓ	11 ⓐ ⓑ ⓒ ⓓ			
	12 ⓕ ⓖ ⓗ ⓙ	12 ⓕ ⓖ ⓗ ⓙ			
	13 ⓐ ⓑ ⓒ ⓓ	13 ⓐ ⓑ ⓒ ⓓ			
	14 ⓕ ⓖ ⓗ ⓙ	14 ⓕ ⓖ ⓗ ⓙ			
	15 ⓐ ⓑ ⓒ ⓓ	15 ⓐ ⓑ ⓒ ⓓ			
	16 ⓕ ⓖ ⓗ ⓙ	16 ⓕ ⓖ ⓗ ⓙ			
	17 ⓐ ⓑ ⓒ ⓓ	17 ⓐ ⓑ ⓒ ⓓ			
	18 ⓕ ⓖ ⓗ ⓙ	18 ⓕ ⓖ ⓗ ⓙ			

Capitalization page_____	Grammar page_____	Sentences page_____	Reference page_____		
1 ⓐ ⓑ ⓒ ⓓ	1 ⓐ ⓑ ⓒ ⓓ	1 ⓐ ⓑ ⓒ ⓓ	1 ⓐ ⓑ ⓒ ⓓ		
2 ⓕ ⓖ ⓗ ⓙ	2 ⓕ ⓖ ⓗ ⓙ	2 ⓕ ⓖ ⓗ ⓙ	2 ⓕ ⓖ ⓗ ⓙ		
3 ⓐ ⓑ ⓒ ⓓ	3 ⓐ ⓑ ⓒ ⓓ	3 ⓐ ⓑ ⓒ ⓓ	3 ⓐ ⓑ ⓒ ⓓ		
4 ⓕ ⓖ ⓗ ⓙ	4 ⓕ ⓖ ⓗ ⓙ	4 ⓕ ⓖ ⓗ ⓙ	4 ⓕ ⓖ ⓗ ⓙ		
5 ⓐ ⓑ ⓒ ⓓ	5 ⓐ ⓑ ⓒ ⓓ	5 ⓐ ⓑ ⓒ ⓓ	5 ⓐ ⓑ ⓒ ⓓ		
6 ⓕ ⓖ ⓗ ⓙ	6 ⓕ ⓖ ⓗ ⓙ	6 ⓕ ⓖ ⓗ ⓙ	6 ⓕ ⓖ ⓗ ⓙ		
7 ⓐ ⓑ ⓒ ⓓ	7 ⓐ ⓑ ⓒ ⓓ	7 ⓐ ⓑ ⓒ ⓓ	7 ⓐ ⓑ ⓒ ⓓ		
8 ⓕ ⓖ ⓗ ⓙ	8 ⓕ ⓖ ⓗ ⓙ	8 ⓕ ⓖ ⓗ ⓙ	8 ⓕ ⓖ ⓗ ⓙ		
9 ⓐ ⓑ ⓒ ⓓ	9 ⓐ ⓑ ⓒ ⓓ	9 ⓐ ⓑ ⓒ ⓓ	9 ⓐ ⓑ ⓒ ⓓ		
10 ⓕ ⓖ ⓗ ⓙ	10 ⓕ ⓖ ⓗ ⓙ	10 ⓕ ⓖ ⓗ ⓙ	10 ⓕ ⓖ ⓗ ⓙ		

Name________________________________ **Answer Sheet-Comprehension**

Narrative page_____	Expository page_____	Directions page_____	Charts page_____	Letters page_____	Poetry page_____
1 ⓐ ⓑ ⓒ ⓓ	1 ⓐ ⓑ ⓒ ⓓ	1 ⓐ ⓑ ⓒ ⓓ	1 ⓐ ⓑ ⓒ ⓓ	1 ⓐ ⓑ ⓒ ⓓ	1 ⓐ ⓑ ⓒ ⓓ
2 ⓕ ⓖ ⓗ ⓙ	2 ⓕ ⓖ ⓗ ⓙ	2 ⓕ ⓖ ⓗ ⓙ	2 ⓕ ⓖ ⓗ ⓙ	2 ⓕ ⓖ ⓗ ⓙ	2 ⓕ ⓖ ⓗ ⓙ
3 ⓐ ⓑ ⓒ ⓓ	3 ⓐ ⓑ ⓒ ⓓ	3 ⓐ ⓑ ⓒ ⓓ	3 ⓐ ⓑ ⓒ ⓓ	3 ⓐ ⓑ ⓒ ⓓ	3 ⓐ ⓑ ⓒ ⓓ
4 ⓕ ⓖ ⓗ ⓙ	4 ⓕ ⓖ ⓗ ⓙ	4 ⓕ ⓖ ⓗ ⓙ	4 ⓕ ⓖ ⓗ ⓙ	4 ⓕ ⓖ ⓗ ⓙ	4 ⓕ ⓖ ⓗ ⓙ
5 ⓐ ⓑ ⓒ ⓓ	5 ⓐ ⓑ ⓒ ⓓ	5 ⓐ ⓑ ⓒ ⓓ	5 ⓐ ⓑ ⓒ ⓓ		5 ⓐ ⓑ ⓒ ⓓ
6 ⓕ ⓖ ⓗ ⓙ	6 ⓕ ⓖ ⓗ ⓙ	6 ⓕ ⓖ ⓗ ⓙ	6 ⓕ ⓖ ⓗ ⓙ		6 ⓕ ⓖ ⓗ ⓙ
					7 ⓐ ⓑ ⓒ ⓓ
					8 ⓕ ⓖ ⓗ ⓙ

Narrative page_____	Expository page_____	Directions page_____	Charts page_____	Letters page_____	Poetry page_____
1 ⓐ ⓑ ⓒ ⓓ	1 ⓐ ⓑ ⓒ ⓓ	1 ⓐ ⓑ ⓒ ⓓ	1 ⓐ ⓑ ⓒ ⓓ	1 ⓐ ⓑ ⓒ ⓓ	1 ⓐ ⓑ ⓒ ⓓ
2 ⓕ ⓖ ⓗ ⓙ	2 ⓕ ⓖ ⓗ ⓙ	2 ⓕ ⓖ ⓗ ⓙ	2 ⓕ ⓖ ⓗ ⓙ	2 ⓕ ⓖ ⓗ ⓙ	2 ⓕ ⓖ ⓗ ⓙ
3 ⓐ ⓑ ⓒ ⓓ	3 ⓐ ⓑ ⓒ ⓓ	3 ⓐ ⓑ ⓒ ⓓ	3 ⓐ ⓑ ⓒ ⓓ	3 ⓐ ⓑ ⓒ ⓓ	3 ⓐ ⓑ ⓒ ⓓ
4 ⓕ ⓖ ⓗ ⓙ	4 ⓕ ⓖ ⓗ ⓙ	4 ⓕ ⓖ ⓗ ⓙ	4 ⓕ ⓖ ⓗ ⓙ	4 ⓕ ⓖ ⓗ ⓙ	4 ⓕ ⓖ ⓗ ⓙ
5 ⓐ ⓑ ⓒ ⓓ	5 ⓐ ⓑ ⓒ ⓓ	5 ⓐ ⓑ ⓒ ⓓ	5 ⓐ ⓑ ⓒ ⓓ		5 ⓐ ⓑ ⓒ ⓓ
6 ⓕ ⓖ ⓗ ⓙ	6 ⓕ ⓖ ⓗ ⓙ	6 ⓕ ⓖ ⓗ ⓙ	6 ⓕ ⓖ ⓗ ⓙ		6 ⓕ ⓖ ⓗ ⓙ
					7 ⓐ ⓑ ⓒ ⓓ
					8 ⓕ ⓖ ⓗ ⓙ

Name______________________________ **Answer Sheet-Word Skills**

Analogies page_____	Syllables page_____	Spelling page_____	Synonyms page_____	Homophones page_____	Vocabulary page_____
1 (a) (b) (c) (d)	1 (a) (b) (c) (d)	1 (a) (b) (c) (d)	1 (a) (b) (c) (d)	1 (a) (b) (c) (d)	1 (a) (b) (c) (d)
2 (f) (g) (h) (j)	2 (f) (g) (h) (j)	2 (f) (g) (h) (j)	2 (f) (g) (h) (j)	2 (f) (g) (h) (j)	2 (f) (g) (h) (j)
3 (a) (b) (c) (d)	3 (a) (b) (c) (d)	3 (a) (b) (c) (d)	3 (a) (b) (c) (d)	3 (a) (b) (c) (d)	3 (a) (b) (c) (d)
4 (f) (g) (h) (j)	4 (f) (g) (h) (j)	4 (f) (g) (h) (j)	4 (f) (g) (h) (j)	4 (f) (g) (h) (j)	4 (f) (g) (h) (j)
5 (a) (b) (c) (d)	5 (a) (b) (c) (d)	5 (a) (b) (c) (d)	5 (a) (b) (c) (d)	5 (a) (b) (c) (d)	5 (a) (b) (c) (d)
6 (f) (g) (h) (j)	6 (f) (g) (h) (j)	6 (f) (g) (h) (j)	6 (f) (g) (h) (j)	6 (f) (g) (h) (j)	6 (f) (g) (h) (j)
7 (a) (b) (c) (d)	7 (a) (b) (c) (d)	7 (a) (b) (c) (d)	7 (a) (b) (c) (d)	7 (a) (b) (c) (d)	7 (a) (b) (c) (d)
8 (f) (g) (h) (j)	8 (f) (g) (h) (j)	8 (f) (g) (h) (j)	8 (f) (g) (h) (j)	8 (f) (g) (h) (j)	8 (f) (g) (h) (j)
9 (a) (b) (c) (d)	9 (a) (b) (c) (d)	9 (a) (b) (c) (d)	9 (a) (b) (c) (d)	9 (a) (b) (c) (d)	9 (a) (b) (c) (d)
10 (f) (g) (h) (j)	10 (f) (g) (h) (j)	10 (f) (g) (h) (j)	10 (f) (g) (h) (j)	10 (f) (g) (h) (j)	10 (f) (g) (h) (j)
	11 (a) (b) (c) (d)	11 (a) (b) (c) (d)			
	12 (f) (g) (h) (j)	12 (f) (g) (h) (j)			
	13 (a) (b) (c) (d)	13 (a) (b) (c) (d)			
	14 (f) (g) (h) (j)	14 (f) (g) (h) (j)			
	15 (a) (b) (c) (d)	15 (a) (b) (c) (d)			
	16 (f) (g) (h) (j)	16 (f) (g) (h) (j)			
	17 (a) (b) (c) (d)	17 (a) (b) (c) (d)			
	18 (f) (g) (h) (j)	18 (f) (g) (h) (j)			

Capitalization page_____	Grammar page_____	Sentences page_____	Reference page_____		
1 (a) (b) (c) (d)	1 (a) (b) (c) (d)	1 (a) (b) (c) (d)	1 (a) (b) (c) (d)		
2 (f) (g) (h) (j)	2 (f) (g) (h) (j)	2 (f) (g) (h) (j)	2 (f) (g) (h) (j)		
3 (a) (b) (c) (d)	3 (a) (b) (c) (d)	3 (a) (b) (c) (d)	3 (a) (b) (c) (d)		
4 (f) (g) (h) (j)	4 (f) (g) (h) (j)	4 (f) (g) (h) (j)	4 (f) (g) (h) (j)		
5 (a) (b) (c) (d)	5 (a) (b) (c) (d)	5 (a) (b) (c) (d)	5 (a) (b) (c) (d)		
6 (f) (g) (h) (j)	6 (f) (g) (h) (j)	6 (f) (g) (h) (j)	6 (f) (g) (h) (j)		
7 (a) (b) (c) (d)	7 (a) (b) (c) (d)	7 (a) (b) (c) (d)	7 (a) (b) (c) (d)		
8 (f) (g) (h) (j)	8 (f) (g) (h) (j)	8 (f) (g) (h) (j)	8 (f) (g) (h) (j)		
9 (a) (b) (c) (d)	9 (a) (b) (c) (d)	9 (a) (b) (c) (d)	9 (a) (b) (c) (d)		
10 (f) (g) (h) (j)	10 (f) (g) (h) (j)	10 (f) (g) (h) (j)	10 (f) (g) (h) (j)		

Name________________________________ **Answer Sheet-Comprehension**

Narrative page_____	Expository page_____	Directions page_____	Charts page_____	Letters page_____	Poetry page_____
1 ⓐ ⓑ ⓒ ⓓ	1 ⓐ ⓑ ⓒ ⓓ	1 ⓐ ⓑ ⓒ ⓓ	1 ⓐ ⓑ ⓒ ⓓ	1 ⓐ ⓑ ⓒ ⓓ	1 ⓐ ⓑ ⓒ ⓓ
2 ⓕ ⓖ ⓗ ⓙ	2 ⓕ ⓖ ⓗ ⓙ	2 ⓕ ⓖ ⓗ ⓙ	2 ⓕ ⓖ ⓗ ⓙ	2 ⓕ ⓖ ⓗ ⓙ	2 ⓕ ⓖ ⓗ ⓙ
3 ⓐ ⓑ ⓒ ⓓ	3 ⓐ ⓑ ⓒ ⓓ	3 ⓐ ⓑ ⓒ ⓓ	3 ⓐ ⓑ ⓒ ⓓ	3 ⓐ ⓑ ⓒ ⓓ	3 ⓐ ⓑ ⓒ ⓓ
4 ⓕ ⓖ ⓗ ⓙ	4 ⓕ ⓖ ⓗ ⓙ	4 ⓕ ⓖ ⓗ ⓙ	4 ⓕ ⓖ ⓗ ⓙ	4 ⓕ ⓖ ⓗ ⓙ	4 ⓕ ⓖ ⓗ ⓙ
5 ⓐ ⓑ ⓒ ⓓ	5 ⓐ ⓑ ⓒ ⓓ	5 ⓐ ⓑ ⓒ ⓓ	5 ⓐ ⓑ ⓒ ⓓ		5 ⓐ ⓑ ⓒ ⓓ
6 ⓕ ⓖ ⓗ ⓙ	6 ⓕ ⓖ ⓗ ⓙ	6 ⓕ ⓖ ⓗ ⓙ	6 ⓕ ⓖ ⓗ ⓙ		6 ⓕ ⓖ ⓗ ⓙ
					7 ⓐ ⓑ ⓒ ⓓ
					8 ⓕ ⓖ ⓗ ⓙ

Narrative page_____	Expository page_____	Directions page_____	Charts page_____	Letters page_____	Poetry page_____
1 ⓐ ⓑ ⓒ ⓓ	1 ⓐ ⓑ ⓒ ⓓ	1 ⓐ ⓑ ⓒ ⓓ	1 ⓐ ⓑ ⓒ ⓓ	1 ⓐ ⓑ ⓒ ⓓ	1 ⓐ ⓑ ⓒ ⓓ
2 ⓕ ⓖ ⓗ ⓙ	2 ⓕ ⓖ ⓗ ⓙ	2 ⓕ ⓖ ⓗ ⓙ	2 ⓕ ⓖ ⓗ ⓙ	2 ⓕ ⓖ ⓗ ⓙ	2 ⓕ ⓖ ⓗ ⓙ
3 ⓐ ⓑ ⓒ ⓓ	3 ⓐ ⓑ ⓒ ⓓ	3 ⓐ ⓑ ⓒ ⓓ	3 ⓐ ⓑ ⓒ ⓓ	3 ⓐ ⓑ ⓒ ⓓ	3 ⓐ ⓑ ⓒ ⓓ
4 ⓕ ⓖ ⓗ ⓙ	4 ⓕ ⓖ ⓗ ⓙ	4 ⓕ ⓖ ⓗ ⓙ	4 ⓕ ⓖ ⓗ ⓙ	4 ⓕ ⓖ ⓗ ⓙ	4 ⓕ ⓖ ⓗ ⓙ
5 ⓐ ⓑ ⓒ ⓓ	5 ⓐ ⓑ ⓒ ⓓ	5 ⓐ ⓑ ⓒ ⓓ	5 ⓐ ⓑ ⓒ ⓓ		5 ⓐ ⓑ ⓒ ⓓ
6 ⓕ ⓖ ⓗ ⓙ	6 ⓕ ⓖ ⓗ ⓙ	6 ⓕ ⓖ ⓗ ⓙ	6 ⓕ ⓖ ⓗ ⓙ		6 ⓕ ⓖ ⓗ ⓙ
					7 ⓐ ⓑ ⓒ ⓓ
					8 ⓕ ⓖ ⓗ ⓙ

Name______________________________ **Answer Sheet-Word Skills**

Analogies page_____	Syllables page_____	Spelling page_____	Synonyms page_____	Homophones page_____	Vocabulary page_____
1 a b c d	1 a b c d	1 a b c d	1 a b c d	1 a b c d	1 a b c d
2 f g h j	2 f g h j	2 f g h j	2 f g h j	2 f g h j	2 f g h j
3 a b c d	3 a b c d	3 a b c d	3 a b c d	3 a b c d	3 a b c d
4 f g h j	4 f g h j	4 f g h j	4 f g h j	4 f g h j	4 f g h j
5 a b c d	5 a b c d	5 a b c d	5 a b c d	5 a b c d	5 a b c d
6 f g h j	6 f g h j	6 f g h j	6 f g h j	6 f g h j	6 f g h j
7 a b c d	7 a b c d	7 a b c d	7 a b c d	7 a b c d	7 a b c d
8 f g h j	8 f g h j	8 f g h j	8 f g h j	8 f g h j	8 f g h j
9 a b c d	9 a b c d	9 a b c d	9 a b c d	9 a b c d	9 a b c d
10 f g h j	10 f g h j	10 f g h j	10 f g h j	10 f g h j	10 f g h j
	11 a b c d	11 a b c d			
	12 f g h j	12 f g h j			
	13 a b c d	13 a b c d			
	14 f g h j	14 f g h j			
	15 a b c d	15 a b c d			
	16 f g h j	16 f g h j			
	17 a b c d	17 a b c d			
	18 f g h j	18 f g h j			

Capitalization page_____	Grammar page_____	Sentences page_____	Reference page_____		
1 a b c d	1 a b c d	1 a b c d	1 a b c d		
2 f g h j	2 f g h j	2 f g h j	2 f g h j		
3 a b c d	3 a b c d	3 a b c d	3 a b c d		
4 f g h j	4 f g h j	4 f g h j	4 f g h j		
5 a b c d	5 a b c d	5 a b c d	5 a b c d		
6 f g h j	6 f g h j	6 f g h j	6 f g h j		
7 a b c d	7 a b c d	7 a b c d	7 a b c d		
8 f g h j	8 f g h j	8 f g h j	8 f g h j		
9 a b c d	9 a b c d	9 a b c d	9 a b c d		
10 f g h j	10 f g h j	10 f g h j	10 f g h j		

Name________________________________ **Answer Sheet-Comprehension**

Narrative page_____	Expository page_____	Directions page_____	Charts page_____	Letters page_____	Poetry page_____
1 ⓐ ⓑ ⓒ ⓓ	1 ⓐ ⓑ ⓒ ⓓ	1 ⓐ ⓑ ⓒ ⓓ	1 ⓐ ⓑ ⓒ ⓓ	1 ⓐ ⓑ ⓒ ⓓ	1 ⓐ ⓑ ⓒ ⓓ
2 ⓕ ⓖ ⓗ ⓙ	2 ⓕ ⓖ ⓗ ⓙ	2 ⓕ ⓖ ⓗ ⓙ	2 ⓕ ⓖ ⓗ ⓙ	2 ⓕ ⓖ ⓗ ⓙ	2 ⓕ ⓖ ⓗ ⓙ
3 ⓐ ⓑ ⓒ ⓓ	3 ⓐ ⓑ ⓒ ⓓ	3 ⓐ ⓑ ⓒ ⓓ	3 ⓐ ⓑ ⓒ ⓓ	3 ⓐ ⓑ ⓒ ⓓ	3 ⓐ ⓑ ⓒ ⓓ
4 ⓕ ⓖ ⓗ ⓙ	4 ⓕ ⓖ ⓗ ⓙ	4 ⓕ ⓖ ⓗ ⓙ	4 ⓕ ⓖ ⓗ ⓙ	4 ⓕ ⓖ ⓗ ⓙ	4 ⓕ ⓖ ⓗ ⓙ
5 ⓐ ⓑ ⓒ ⓓ	5 ⓐ ⓑ ⓒ ⓓ	5 ⓐ ⓑ ⓒ ⓓ	5 ⓐ ⓑ ⓒ ⓓ		5 ⓐ ⓑ ⓒ ⓓ
6 ⓕ ⓖ ⓗ ⓙ	6 ⓕ ⓖ ⓗ ⓙ	6 ⓕ ⓖ ⓗ ⓙ	6 ⓕ ⓖ ⓗ ⓙ		6 ⓕ ⓖ ⓗ ⓙ
					7 ⓐ ⓑ ⓒ ⓓ
					8 ⓕ ⓖ ⓗ ⓙ

Narrative page_____	Expository page_____	Directions page_____	Charts page_____	Letters page_____	Poetry page_____
1 ⓐ ⓑ ⓒ ⓓ	1 ⓐ ⓑ ⓒ ⓓ	1 ⓐ ⓑ ⓒ ⓓ	1 ⓐ ⓑ ⓒ ⓓ	1 ⓐ ⓑ ⓒ ⓓ	1 ⓐ ⓑ ⓒ ⓓ
2 ⓕ ⓖ ⓗ ⓙ	2 ⓕ ⓖ ⓗ ⓙ	2 ⓕ ⓖ ⓗ ⓙ	2 ⓕ ⓖ ⓗ ⓙ	2 ⓕ ⓖ ⓗ ⓙ	2 ⓕ ⓖ ⓗ ⓙ
3 ⓐ ⓑ ⓒ ⓓ	3 ⓐ ⓑ ⓒ ⓓ	3 ⓐ ⓑ ⓒ ⓓ	3 ⓐ ⓑ ⓒ ⓓ	3 ⓐ ⓑ ⓒ ⓓ	3 ⓐ ⓑ ⓒ ⓓ
4 ⓕ ⓖ ⓗ ⓙ	4 ⓕ ⓖ ⓗ ⓙ	4 ⓕ ⓖ ⓗ ⓙ	4 ⓕ ⓖ ⓗ ⓙ	4 ⓕ ⓖ ⓗ ⓙ	4 ⓕ ⓖ ⓗ ⓙ
5 ⓐ ⓑ ⓒ ⓓ	5 ⓐ ⓑ ⓒ ⓓ	5 ⓐ ⓑ ⓒ ⓓ	5 ⓐ ⓑ ⓒ ⓓ		5 ⓐ ⓑ ⓒ ⓓ
6 ⓕ ⓖ ⓗ ⓙ	6 ⓕ ⓖ ⓗ ⓙ	6 ⓕ ⓖ ⓗ ⓙ	6 ⓕ ⓖ ⓗ ⓙ		6 ⓕ ⓖ ⓗ ⓙ
					7 ⓐ ⓑ ⓒ ⓓ
					8 ⓕ ⓖ ⓗ ⓙ

Name________________________________ **Answer Sheet-Word Skills**

Analogies
page_____

1 ⓐ ⓑ ⓒ ⓓ
2 ⓕ ⓖ ⓗ ⓙ
3 ⓐ ⓑ ⓒ ⓓ
4 ⓕ ⓖ ⓗ ⓙ
5 ⓐ ⓑ ⓒ ⓓ
6 ⓕ ⓖ ⓗ ⓙ
7 ⓐ ⓑ ⓒ ⓓ
8 ⓕ ⓖ ⓗ ⓙ
9 ⓐ ⓑ ⓒ ⓓ
10 ⓕ ⓖ ⓗ ⓙ

Syllables
page_____

1 ⓐ ⓑ ⓒ ⓓ
2 ⓕ ⓖ ⓗ ⓙ
3 ⓐ ⓑ ⓒ ⓓ
4 ⓕ ⓖ ⓗ ⓙ
5 ⓐ ⓑ ⓒ ⓓ
6 ⓕ ⓖ ⓗ ⓙ
7 ⓐ ⓑ ⓒ ⓓ
8 ⓕ ⓖ ⓗ ⓙ
9 ⓐ ⓑ ⓒ ⓓ
10 ⓕ ⓖ ⓗ ⓙ
11 ⓐ ⓑ ⓒ ⓓ
12 ⓕ ⓖ ⓗ ⓙ
13 ⓐ ⓑ ⓒ ⓓ
14 ⓕ ⓖ ⓗ ⓙ
15 ⓐ ⓑ ⓒ ⓓ
16 ⓕ ⓖ ⓗ ⓙ
17 ⓐ ⓑ ⓒ ⓓ
18 ⓕ ⓖ ⓗ ⓙ

Spelling
page_____

1 ⓐ ⓑ ⓒ ⓓ
2 ⓕ ⓖ ⓗ ⓙ
3 ⓐ ⓑ ⓒ ⓓ
4 ⓕ ⓖ ⓗ ⓙ
5 ⓐ ⓑ ⓒ ⓓ
6 ⓕ ⓖ ⓗ ⓙ
7 ⓐ ⓑ ⓒ ⓓ
8 ⓕ ⓖ ⓗ ⓙ
9 ⓐ ⓑ ⓒ ⓓ
10 ⓕ ⓖ ⓗ ⓙ
11 ⓐ ⓑ ⓒ ⓓ
12 ⓕ ⓖ ⓗ ⓙ
13 ⓐ ⓑ ⓒ ⓓ
14 ⓕ ⓖ ⓗ ⓙ
15 ⓐ ⓑ ⓒ ⓓ
16 ⓕ ⓖ ⓗ ⓙ
17 ⓐ ⓑ ⓒ ⓓ
18 ⓕ ⓖ ⓗ ⓙ

Synonyms
page_____

1 ⓐ ⓑ ⓒ ⓓ
2 ⓕ ⓖ ⓗ ⓙ
3 ⓐ ⓑ ⓒ ⓓ
4 ⓕ ⓖ ⓗ ⓙ
5 ⓐ ⓑ ⓒ ⓓ
6 ⓕ ⓖ ⓗ ⓙ
7 ⓐ ⓑ ⓒ ⓓ
8 ⓕ ⓖ ⓗ ⓙ
9 ⓐ ⓑ ⓒ ⓓ
10 ⓕ ⓖ ⓗ ⓙ

Homophones
page_____

1 ⓐ ⓑ ⓒ ⓓ
2 ⓕ ⓖ ⓗ ⓙ
3 ⓐ ⓑ ⓒ ⓓ
4 ⓕ ⓖ ⓗ ⓙ
5 ⓐ ⓑ ⓒ ⓓ
6 ⓕ ⓖ ⓗ ⓙ
7 ⓐ ⓑ ⓒ ⓓ
8 ⓕ ⓖ ⓗ ⓙ
9 ⓐ ⓑ ⓒ ⓓ
10 ⓕ ⓖ ⓗ ⓙ

Vocabulary
page_____

1 ⓐ ⓑ ⓒ ⓓ
2 ⓕ ⓖ ⓗ ⓙ
3 ⓐ ⓑ ⓒ ⓓ
4 ⓕ ⓖ ⓗ ⓙ
5 ⓐ ⓑ ⓒ ⓓ
6 ⓕ ⓖ ⓗ ⓙ
7 ⓐ ⓑ ⓒ ⓓ
8 ⓕ ⓖ ⓗ ⓙ
9 ⓐ ⓑ ⓒ ⓓ
10 ⓕ ⓖ ⓗ ⓙ

Capitalization
page_____

1 ⓐ ⓑ ⓒ ⓓ
2 ⓕ ⓖ ⓗ ⓙ
3 ⓐ ⓑ ⓒ ⓓ
4 ⓕ ⓖ ⓗ ⓙ
5 ⓐ ⓑ ⓒ ⓓ
6 ⓕ ⓖ ⓗ ⓙ
7 ⓐ ⓑ ⓒ ⓓ
8 ⓕ ⓖ ⓗ ⓙ
9 ⓐ ⓑ ⓒ ⓓ
10 ⓕ ⓖ ⓗ ⓙ

Grammar
page_____

1 ⓐ ⓑ ⓒ ⓓ
2 ⓕ ⓖ ⓗ ⓙ
3 ⓐ ⓑ ⓒ ⓓ
4 ⓕ ⓖ ⓗ ⓙ
5 ⓐ ⓑ ⓒ ⓓ
6 ⓕ ⓖ ⓗ ⓙ
7 ⓐ ⓑ ⓒ ⓓ
8 ⓕ ⓖ ⓗ ⓙ
9 ⓐ ⓑ ⓒ ⓓ
10 ⓕ ⓖ ⓗ ⓙ

Sentences
page_____

1 ⓐ ⓑ ⓒ ⓓ
2 ⓕ ⓖ ⓗ ⓙ
3 ⓐ ⓑ ⓒ ⓓ
4 ⓕ ⓖ ⓗ ⓙ
5 ⓐ ⓑ ⓒ ⓓ
6 ⓕ ⓖ ⓗ ⓙ
7 ⓐ ⓑ ⓒ ⓓ
8 ⓕ ⓖ ⓗ ⓙ
9 ⓐ ⓑ ⓒ ⓓ
10 ⓕ ⓖ ⓗ ⓙ

Reference
page_____

1 ⓐ ⓑ ⓒ ⓓ
2 ⓕ ⓖ ⓗ ⓙ
3 ⓐ ⓑ ⓒ ⓓ
4 ⓕ ⓖ ⓗ ⓙ
5 ⓐ ⓑ ⓒ ⓓ
6 ⓕ ⓖ ⓗ ⓙ
7 ⓐ ⓑ ⓒ ⓓ
8 ⓕ ⓖ ⓗ ⓙ
9 ⓐ ⓑ ⓒ ⓓ
10 ⓕ ⓖ ⓗ ⓙ

Name________________________________ **Answer Sheet-Comprehension**

Narrative page____	Expository page____	Directions page____	Charts page____	Letters page____	Poetry page____
1 ⓐ ⓑ ⓒ ⓓ	1 ⓐ ⓑ ⓒ ⓓ	1 ⓐ ⓑ ⓒ ⓓ	1 ⓐ ⓑ ⓒ ⓓ	1 ⓐ ⓑ ⓒ ⓓ	1 ⓐ ⓑ ⓒ ⓓ
2 ⓕ ⓖ ⓗ ⓙ	2 ⓕ ⓖ ⓗ ⓙ	2 ⓕ ⓖ ⓗ ⓙ	2 ⓕ ⓖ ⓗ ⓙ	2 ⓕ ⓖ ⓗ ⓙ	2 ⓕ ⓖ ⓗ ⓙ
3 ⓐ ⓑ ⓒ ⓓ	3 ⓐ ⓑ ⓒ ⓓ	3 ⓐ ⓑ ⓒ ⓓ	3 ⓐ ⓑ ⓒ ⓓ	3 ⓐ ⓑ ⓒ ⓓ	3 ⓐ ⓑ ⓒ ⓓ
4 ⓕ ⓖ ⓗ ⓙ	4 ⓕ ⓖ ⓗ ⓙ	4 ⓕ ⓖ ⓗ ⓙ	4 ⓕ ⓖ ⓗ ⓙ	4 ⓕ ⓖ ⓗ ⓙ	4 ⓕ ⓖ ⓗ ⓙ
5 ⓐ ⓑ ⓒ ⓓ	5 ⓐ ⓑ ⓒ ⓓ	5 ⓐ ⓑ ⓒ ⓓ	5 ⓐ ⓑ ⓒ ⓓ		5 ⓐ ⓑ ⓒ ⓓ
6 ⓕ ⓖ ⓗ ⓙ	6 ⓕ ⓖ ⓗ ⓙ	6 ⓕ ⓖ ⓗ ⓙ	6 ⓕ ⓖ ⓗ ⓙ		6 ⓕ ⓖ ⓗ ⓙ
					7 ⓐ ⓑ ⓒ ⓓ
					8 ⓕ ⓖ ⓗ ⓙ

Narrative page____	Expository page____	Directions page____	Charts page____	Letters page____	Poetry page____
1 ⓐ ⓑ ⓒ ⓓ	1 ⓐ ⓑ ⓒ ⓓ	1 ⓐ ⓑ ⓒ ⓓ	1 ⓐ ⓑ ⓒ ⓓ	1 ⓐ ⓑ ⓒ ⓓ	1 ⓐ ⓑ ⓒ ⓓ
2 ⓕ ⓖ ⓗ ⓙ	2 ⓕ ⓖ ⓗ ⓙ	2 ⓕ ⓖ ⓗ ⓙ	2 ⓕ ⓖ ⓗ ⓙ	2 ⓕ ⓖ ⓗ ⓙ	2 ⓕ ⓖ ⓗ ⓙ
3 ⓐ ⓑ ⓒ ⓓ	3 ⓐ ⓑ ⓒ ⓓ	3 ⓐ ⓑ ⓒ ⓓ	3 ⓐ ⓑ ⓒ ⓓ	3 ⓐ ⓑ ⓒ ⓓ	3 ⓐ ⓑ ⓒ ⓓ
4 ⓕ ⓖ ⓗ ⓙ	4 ⓕ ⓖ ⓗ ⓙ	4 ⓕ ⓖ ⓗ ⓙ	4 ⓕ ⓖ ⓗ ⓙ	4 ⓕ ⓖ ⓗ ⓙ	4 ⓕ ⓖ ⓗ ⓙ
5 ⓐ ⓑ ⓒ ⓓ	5 ⓐ ⓑ ⓒ ⓓ	5 ⓐ ⓑ ⓒ ⓓ	5 ⓐ ⓑ ⓒ ⓓ		5 ⓐ ⓑ ⓒ ⓓ
6 ⓕ ⓖ ⓗ ⓙ	6 ⓕ ⓖ ⓗ ⓙ	6 ⓕ ⓖ ⓗ ⓙ	6 ⓕ ⓖ ⓗ ⓙ		6 ⓕ ⓖ ⓗ ⓙ
					7 ⓐ ⓑ ⓒ ⓓ
					8 ⓕ ⓖ ⓗ ⓙ

accomplice

acute

ample

apparition

apprehensive

attachment

audition

bewildering

chafing

chasm

clarity

comical

comprehend

compromise

contempt

contradict

conviction 	decade 	dedicate 	detach
disarray 	domestic 	emit 	emphasize
exertion 	expanse 	exploit 	famine
fledgling 	fraud 	furtive 	futile

grimace © CD-3739	grubby © CD-3739	hamper © CD-3739	hark © CD-3739
hence © CD-3739	hermit © CD-3739	impatient © CD-3739	incredulous © CD-3739
indignation © CD-3739	ingenious © CD-3739	intervene © CD-3739	intruder © CD-3739
invalid © CD-3739	legacy © CD-3739	literal © CD-3739	manuscript © CD-3739

merit	nominate	nonchalant	obstinate
omen	omit	paradise	passion
penicillin	perceive	piccolo	potential
precarious	presume	prior	profound

© CD-3739
© CD-3739
© CD-3739
© CD-3739
© CD-3739
© CD-3739
© CD-3739
© CD-3739
© CD-3739
© CD-3739
© CD-3739
© CD-3739
© CD-3739
© CD-3739
© CD-3739

provoke 	**random** 	**recede** 	**replica**
resemblance 	**ruddy** 	**rueful** 	**sarcasm**
semester 	**semicircle** 	**sentiment** 	**significant**
simultaneous 	**skirmish** 	**slumber** 	**spasm**

speculate 	spontaneous 	strenuous 	submerge
summarize 	supervise 	symbolize 	tedious
turret 	tutor 	unanimous 	unison
verify 	vicinity 	vocal 	void